W0082468

Organizing Knowledge for Environmentally and Socially Sustainable Development

Proceedings of a Concurrent Meeting
of the Fifth Annual World Bank Conference
on Environmentally and Socially
Sustainable Development,
"Partnerships for Global Ecosystem Management:
Science, Economics and Law"

*Cosponsored by UNESCO and the World Bank
and held at the World Bank
Washington, D.C., October 9–10, 1997*

*Ismail Serageldin, Tariq Husain, Joan Martin-Brown,
Gustavo López Ospina, and Jeanne Damlamian, Editors*

*The World Bank
Washington, D.C.*

This report has been prepared by the staff of the World Bank. The judgments expressed do not necessarily reflect the views of the Board of Executive Directors or of the governments they represent.

Cover photograph by Curt Carnemark. Mosque detail, Morocco.

Ismail Serageldin is vice president, Special Programs; Tariq Husain is senior advisor, Capacity Building, Operational Core Services; and Joan Martin-Brown is adviser to the vice president for Special Programs, all at the World Bank. Gustavo López Ospina is director, Transdisciplinary Project on Educating for a Sustainable Future, and Jeanne Damlamian is senior programme specialist, Transdisciplinary Project on Educating for a Sustainable Future, both at the United Nations Educational, Scientific and Cultural Organisation (UNESCO).

Library of Congress Cataloging-in-Publication Data

International Conference on Environmentally Sustainable Development
  (5th : 1997 : World Bank)
    Organizing knowledge for environmentally and socially sustainable
  development : proceedings of a concurrent meeting of the fifth
  annual World Bank Conference on Environmentally and Socially
  Sustainable Development / Ismail Serageldin, ... [et al.], editors.
      p.   cm. — (Environmentally and socially sustainable
  development)
    ISBN 0-8213-4250-9
    1. Sustainable development—Research—Congresses.   I. Serageldin,
  Ismail, 1944–   . II. Title.   IV. Series: Environmentally and
  socially sustainable development series.
  HC79.E5I5333   1998
  333.7'07'2—dc21   98-3988
                                                          CIP

The text and the cover are printed on recycled paper, with a flood aqueous coating on the cover.

Contents

Preface

The United Nations Educational, Scientific and Cultural Organisation (UNESCO) and the World Bank cosponsored this event to engage academic and development leaders in considering the requirements for organizing and linking knowledge, research, and disciplines to appropriately respond to the challenges of environmentally and socially sustainable development (ESSD).

Faculty and scholars from higher education, including the schools of law, economics, international relations, business, public administration, natural resources and the environment, and natural and social sciences were invited. Included were members of the Task Force on Higher Education and Society recently convened by UNESCO and the World Bank. The workshop was organized as a Concurrent Meeting of the Fifth Annual World Bank Conference on ESSD.

Rationale

The World Bank is undergoing a transformation in its organizational arrangements and mission. Two requirements of this effort are to improve the integration of cutting-edge knowledge in Bank operations, and to mainstream social and environmental concerns in the Bank's development financing. Key to both efforts is establishing institutional processes that link knowledge and practice. UNESCO, an institution devoted to education and the environmental sciences for over fifty years, is also working to come to grips with the intellectual and organizational demands of sustainability. The challenges are formidable, including reorienting formal education systems at all levels, mobilizing all sectors of society behind education as an indispensable instrument for attaining sustainable development, training nearly 60 million teachers in interdisciplinary approaches, and reaching beyond schools to define education as a lifelong endeavor for people of all ages and from all walks of life.

For the World Bank, UNESCO, other international development institutions, and the United Nations system as a whole, and nations to respond most effectively to the challenges inherent in ESSD, there must be a commitment to develop candidates for employment who are each skilled in a specific discipline, yet who also systematically consider the impact of their expertise on other disciplines and sectors and who are aware of the connections of their disciplines with other areas of specialty. At the same time these actors need to consider how institutions of higher education and research can contribute to developing a citizenry prepared to support sustainability through changes in values and lifestyles—changes that must be based on understanding the issues and what is at stake for the future. This more broadminded, interdisciplinary approach is needed to support environmentally and socially sustainable development.

Key Questions

The two-day meeting addressed four questions related to the academic preparation of those participating in the development and commercial realms through law, economics, business, foreign service, rural development, urban planning, and the natural and social sciences:

1. What are the new content elements and parameters required by the ESSD paradigm in specific disciplines?
2. What content links are necessary among disciplines to ensure that such disciplines explicitly address cross-sectoral requirements in development?
3. What are the research gaps related to implementing ESSD, and how can they be addressed by doctoral and post-doctoral research?
4. How do the disconnects among disciplines affect sustainable development at the national level?

Objectives

The conference had three objectives:

1. To encourage partnerships among the academic, development, and finance communities working in a given field to link disciplines and sectoral initiatives and to avoid economic, social, and ecological liabilities in development processes
2. To encourage graduate research agendas that link disciplines to respond to the challenges of environmentally and socially sustainable development

3. To encourage new initiatives among academic and research organizations, UNESCO, the World Bank, and other international bodies to reorient higher education to address the requirements of environmentally and socially sustainable development.

Conclusion

Developing nations are seeking technology transfer, undertaking new partnerships with the private sector, and pursuing the development of their own scientific and technical capacities. As they do, the quality and content of academic endeavors and research agendas become critical in organizing and investing in knowledge for sustainable development, and in building international networks and partnerships to exchange knowledge and experience. For development to be done differently, those being educated must be empowered to perceive and connect their disciplines differently, and to develop knowledge that will be useful for decisionmakers outside the academic and research worlds.

This conference explored the critical tasks confronting educators and development practitioners, and the need for a new discourse between them. Perhaps among disciplines we need to adopt the principle of porosity. The World Bank and UNESCO remain committed to working in this direction in the future.

Ismail Serageldin
Tariq Husain
Joan Martin-Brown
Jeanne Damlamian
Gustavo López Ospina

Setting the Agenda

Introduction
Tariq Husain

This is an important occasion, with thinking and caring minds from all over the world getting together to consider how to organize knowledge for environmentally sustainable development. The meeting is sponsored jointly by UNESCO and the World Bank's Learning and Leadership Center.

"Sustainability" is a word increasingly in our vocabulary. The goal it reflects is that we follow policies and take actions to ensure that while we try to meet present needs, the needs of future generations are not compromised. This is a very complex, multifaceted objective. It requires the organization of knowledge on an unprecedented scale to enable humankind, or much of humankind, to act sustainably.

The purpose of this meeting is to continue to pursue the critically important task of organizing knowledge that can help address key issues facing all of us. The issues ultimately concern survival, and they concern the well-being of our children and their children.

Specifically, we meet to help further sustainable development that can ensure future generations' social, economic, and personal well-being, creating conditions which allow them to live harmoniously with a protected environment.

Of course, the responsibility for creating these conditions falls on the adults of today, particularly adults who are in a position to do something about it, and who also appreciate the need for doing so. Indeed this room is filled with people who are both aware of the issues and who have the knowledge and the capacity to do something about them.

Some of you were present when we assembled here last year, and some of you are new entrants. Jacques-Yves Cousteau was among us then, and he asked us at that time to assemble again this year and report on what we have accomplished since that meeting.

A Warning to Humanity

For perspective on this immense subject we should also keep in mind some other important events. Think of what happened in 1992, for example: it was not just the Rio conference that was highly significant that year. I have in mind the occasion when about 1,600 scientists jointly declared "A Warning to Mankind." The scientists were from all disciplines and from all parts of the world; more than 100 Nobel laureates signed their names.

We all resonated with this statement. Here is a paragraph from it:

> Human beings and the natural world are on a collision course. Human activities inflict harsh and often irreversible damage on the environment and on critical resources. If not checked, many of our current practices put at risk the future that we wish for human society and the plant and animal kingdoms, and may so alter the living world that it will be unable to sustain life in the manner that we know. Fundamental changes are urgent, if we are to avoid the collision our present course will bring about.

That was a very large group of very bright, caring minds expressing a deep concern. We might ask, has there been any progress since? As Jacques-Yves Cousteau might ask, what have we accomplished—we in this room, and we, the human race?

In fact there has been forward movement. The progress has not been comprehensive, but yet it is still noteworthy. For instance, about 100 developing countries have now prepared national environmental strategies setting priorities for action. Of course, the implementation of these action plans will require knowledge and capacity. That is where educators and leaders are needed. They will help achieve the implementing capacity for these plans and help ensure that the priorities are being chosen correctly.

One hundred forty-three developing countries have ratified the Biodiversity Convention. That is considerable progress. Someone must help weigh the tradeoffs that face humankind as these actions are implemented. Someone must understand the public support that is needed for the benefits that will flow to the children of our children, benefits that may be treasures not just because they contribute to biodiversity, and to which no one has prior or exclusive claim.

Other signs of progress include the fact that 138 countries have ratified the framework Convention on Climate Change. In addition 119 have ratified the Montreal Protocol of the Vienna Convention to protect the stratospheric ozone layer. Meanwhile, the World Bank launched the Global Environmental Facility in 1994 in collaboration with many countries of the world, along with taking other joint environmental steps.

Much to Do

All of these measures add up to a very modest beginning. A great deal remains to be done, as pointed out by our president, Mr. James D. Wolfensohn, when he gave the opening address to the overall World Bank conference on environmentally and socially sustainable development earlier this week. For the purposes of our discussion here, let me list several of the points he made:
- In terms of factors posing major claims on the environment, we see the need for doubling agricultural production in the next thirty-five years; global energy use is expected to double as well.
- We are already taxing the productivity of Earth's natural systems, including the oceans. Imagine the consequences of these additional environmental stresses and the need for science, mitigation actions, and development of less environmentally stressful alternatives in order for sustainability to be a viable option for the future.
- Pollution continues to worsen in many cities of the developing world, with 1.3 billion people affected. This situation carries severe implications for health, productivity, and for the overall quality of life for these people.
- The lost productivity of soil in many African countries has been estimated to cost 3 to 5 percent of their GDP. Some of this soil damage is irreversible.
- Depletion and pollution of water—a basic resource—has caused the real cost of providing drinking water to quadruple in many areas. Food costs are being similarly affected.
- Relating to biodiversity, species continue to be lost at a level between 1,000 to 10,000 times the natural extinction rate.
- The world's carbon emissions have increased 60 percent over the last 25 years. If action is not taken to control them, they will increase by about 60 or 70 percent more in the next 25 years.

All of these figures may be familiar to this audience, but for many of the world's leaders and for much of the rest of humankind they are not. Here again is an education function, one which needs to be carried out with great conviction and passion.

Need for Partnerships

Such huge issues are involved, however, that no single institution, country, or discipline can do the job. There is the need for partnership, a need that is being emphasized by the World Bank, and that was reiterated by our president at a global conference in Hong Kong and in Mr. Wolfensohn's opening address earlier this week at the overall conference of which this meeting is a part.

Such a partnership concerns the acquisition and sharing of knowledge in the largest sense of the word, across disciplinary boundaries. The knowledge regards problems, but it also regards solutions.

The challenge that we have in this community, and in the community that we represent outside these rooms, is to educate students from all parts of the world, those who are not only young, but the ones who are already working in the world, mostly as adults.

The task is to systematize the existing knowledge base and share it widely, using all the powers of modern technology, made possible by its plummeting costs. Indeed technology has created great educational possibilities, but will and action are necessary, too.

Our agenda at this meeting and beyond is to address critical questions related to the academic preparations of the students I have referred to, including those in the process of developing their own capacity to study, teach, and provide advice. Explaining our challenge, I borrow here several items from the statement by the 1,600 scientists to which I referred earlier. It is in their warning and advice that we can find invaluable guidance as to what we collectively need to do now, tomorrow, and the day after.

Ideas for an Agenda

What follows are issues that the scientists said are targets of concern and attention. Of course, this is just a sampling from their statements:

1. Global and local environmental change and its causes, including poverty, population growth, government policies, and policies to mitigate effects.
2. Providing advice on, and a study of, the conditions for human development in the largest sense of the word, in which each one of us is helped to reach our potential, particularly considering the impediments that result from social inequality, and the other biases that exist in the world, based on differences that shouldn't matter, such as ethnicity, color, gender, income level, and religion. It is the totality of human economics, that knows no boundaries, that must be studied and addressed.

3. Improved mechanisms for building indigenous capacity in the natural sciences and, importantly, an integrated, interdisciplinary assessment of societal issues. The point is that there are boundaries between disciplines that will need to be crossed in a very deep and systematic way.
4. The study of technologies and the strategies for sustainable development. In understanding the importance of this item, we need only recall the heavy additional claims that will be placed on natural ecosystems just to feed the world and provide the water that it will drink, given the projected requirements.
5. Networks, treaties, and conventions to protect the global commons—overall, a very different, interactive kind of relationship across national boundaries, so that we can protect the global commons for today and tomorrow.
6. Worldwide exchanges of scientists in education, training, and research—another indication of the need to share and broaden our knowledge base. There is no alternative but to see the condition of the world and its people as a common problem and to solve it together.

A Call for a Global Ethic

We should point out that technical excellence by itself will not meet these challenges. Boundaries must be crossed into areas from which we can draw more energy, particularly in the domain of values and ethics. For instance it is very important in our educational institutions to talk about this critically important matter that can enable students, especially the youth of today, to bridge the divisions that separate us unnecessarily, divisions that should exist for purposes of identity only, not for different treatment. I am speaking once more of the dividing lines of ethnicity, color, gender, income level, and religion.

Let me close then, with this emphasis on commonality rather than separation, and I will quote again that significant 1992 statement of the scientists:

A new ethic is required, a new attitude toward discharging our responsibility for caring for ourselves and for the Earth. This ethic must motivate a great movement, convincing sometimes reluctant leaders, governments, and people to effect the needed changes.

We need the help of many people to achieve this vital goal, beginning with scientists and educators, and including business leaders and many others.

The challenge for all of us is to teach not only technical excellence, addressing and advising on relevant issues, but to teach the values that will permit and promote a new global ethic. Without such values, common action and a real sense of common bonds will be very difficult to achieve.

Turning Education Around
Benjamin Ladner

In *The Order of Things* philosopher Michel Foucault cites a passage from Borges in which he quotes "a certain Chinese encyclopedia" to the effect that "animals can be divided into:

A. Belonging to the emperor
B. Embalmed
C. Tame
D. Suckling pigs
E. Sirens
F. Fabulous
G. Stray dogs
H. Included in the present classification
I. Frenzied
J. Innumerable
K. Drawn with a very fine camel hair brush
L. Et cetera
M. Having just broken the water pitcher and
N. That [which] from a long way off looks like flies."

This incredible taxonomy imposes upon us a stark impossibility of thinking this way, not only because these are strange images in odd juxtaposition but also because there is no common ground on which a coming together of these things could be imagined or would be possible.

British-American writer Elizabeth Sewell once described the American academic structure as:

A huge dream mansion, a kind of crazy skyscraper that is continually being added to in all directions—up, down, sideways—a fantastic superstructure of which the materials are theses, dissertations, courses in universities, library lists, articles in learned journals, works of criticism. The whole great building stands entirely on its own. Belief in its own existence as an expert in specialized skill prohibits it from any intercourse with other similar structures. The towers of other disciplines also rise up in isolation all over the place like ziggurats on the sandy plain of Babylon. We are quite familiar with closed worlds of this kind of functioning efficiency, functioning on their own terms, producing plenty of results, only these results make sense inside the system and do not bear relation to whatever is in real life. Maybe it is not a horrid accident, but a logical conclusion of how we think.

A Self-Absorbed Academic Structure

Sewell is raising a fundamental question about the kind of order we have in our academic structures. We have constructed orders of mind that have become orders of inquiry that have spawned institutional structures that perfectly reflect our orders of mind. It is not the content of knowledge but the social and professional organization of knowledge that has been institutionalized in universities and that sets the boundaries of the disciplines of inquiry. The order of these disciplines has mesmerized us for so long that, collectively, we now spend just as much of our institutional resources and time preserving professional prerogatives as we do actually deepening human insight.

Where did this self-absorbing fascination with ideas and structure come from? Eric Heller wrote many years ago in *The Disinherited Mind*:

Common sense in each epoch consists of an astonishingly complex agglomeration of highly sophisticated half-truths. One such half-truth in which our common sense indulges, and much in our higher education is based upon it, is the doctrine that any kind of knowledge, as long as it supplies us with correctly ascertained facts, is worth teaching and learning, and that the more such correct facts we accumulate, the nearer we come to truth.

We are convinced that truth is determined through a plebiscite of facts. The disciplines in which so many of us work and have been trained are really mediating constructions of thought that give pattern, order, and, hence, meaning to our experience. A key question, however, is whether we have so ordered the structure of knowledge that have unwittingly undermined our capacity to hold in our understanding, as well as in our lives, a common experience and a common world.

It may be that what we put between us as mediating structures of thought has severed our sense of our common responsibility for what is *actually* between us. Our tolerance for abstraction as a mediating instrument for violence, deprivation, degradation, indignity, and death has become so familiar and so normal that it is now a global way of life.

There are academics and literary critics, one being George Steiner, who have commented on this extraordinary phenomenon of the impact of high abstraction being translated into high culture that serves as a justification for murder and death. To be specific, it was highly literate guards who, after shoveling Jewish bodies into Nazi ovens, often concluded their day listening to Mozart and reading Rilke.

A major part of our professional task in a new century will be to imagine the shape of new frameworks of knowledge that are congenial not only to our daily habits of thinking, talking, listening, reading, writing, and administering, but also to the larger significance of our lives and world.

A Split in Education and in Living

Of all the ills that presently beset us—social, political, militaristic, and economic—perhaps none is more pernicious than the fragmentation of the academy, which mandates separations between specialization and generalization, between teaching and research, between the arts and the sciences.

Why is this split so pernicious? There are two reasons. One is simply that the divisions are false. Whatever benefits may be claimed in the name of specialization and however securely established are the bureaucratic walls that protect these separate areas, these divisions profoundly misrepresent the real nature of inquiry, and, for that matter, the nature of our experience of reality.

Second, these divisions reflect and perpetuate a fundamental disorientation that marks our cultures. It is a disorientation created by, among other things, our inherited assumption of what knowledge is.

We need not appeal to a complicated epistemology to recognize the seemingly self-evident assumptions in our culture and in our universities that thinking is one thing and feeling is something else, that theory and practice are altogether separate, and that clarity is always closer to truth than ambiguity.

These assumptions, and the institutions that embody them, have deprived us of confidence in our ability to comprehend rightly our own minds, our bodies, and our world, with the result that we have slowly been losing our minds at the same time that we have been losing our world. Yet, Maurice Merleau-Ponty helpfully reminds us that the world is not what we think but what we live through.

Hannah Arendt wrote in *The Human Condition*: "It could be that we will forever be unable to understand, that is to think and speak, about the things which nevertheless we are able to do." This situation has come about, she explains, because the truths of the modern scientific world can be demonstrated only in highly technical and mathematical formulations that do not lend themselves to expression in normal speech and thought.

A Human Crisis

Nevertheless, on the basis of such abstract formulations, we are now able to unleash powerful events into nature that are beyond our ability to understand precisely—either what is happening or what the consequences are for our human lives. In other words we can *do* what we cannot *think*. We can cause to happen what we cannot understand. This signals the possibility of a parting of the ways between knowledge that is *knowing how to*, on the one hand, and knowledge that is *knowing the meaning of*, on the other.

When skills and techniques lose their connection to meaning and significance, there is a human crisis of the first order. This is true whether the setting for the crisis is a second grade classroom or a graduate seminar, or whether a nuclear bomb or a space shuttle is being constructed.

The fact is, as Arendt observes, insofar as we live and move and act in this world, we can experience meaningfulness only because we can talk and make sense of the world to each other. It is not the theoretical formulation of reality that holds the meaning of our lives together: it is common, ordinary, garden-variety speech with our fellow human beings.

My sense is that the divisions in the modern fragmented university between disciplines, schools, colleges, and colleagues have become so intractable, not primarily because of theoretical disagreements or methodological disputes, but because we can no longer talk and make sense to each other in ordinary language about the things that matter most to us.

Loss of a Public Space and Shared Values

When we can no longer recognize what we hold in common as colleagues or as citizens, then in the strictest sense imaginable we have lost our common sense, our sense of what is common to us. It is, after all, what is between us, what is not possessed by any single one of us, that is the basis of a civilized people.

The loss of the commons, the loss of public space where we speak meaningfully to each other despite our private, specialized interests, also reduces our sense of shared values. The disappearance of commonly held values is an indication that there is no compelling image of ourselves as human beings and of our world that we mutually affirm and spontaneously delight in.

When we really come to believe—and we may be perilously close to this now—that what our minds most closely resemble is a computer, and what the world most closely resembles is a machine, then it is no wonder that we can so easily disregard and destroy Earth and our fellow human beings.

There is now a social order, or, some would say, disorder, that has gorged itself on quick-fix solutions and temporary measures for satisfying hollow, weary lives. Sadly, even in our success, even in our academic and technical success, the fact is that on an ordinary Thursday afternoon, sitting in our family rooms, we really do want to know where pain and joy intersect; how time fulfills itself in a single life; what we are working for; how we can make delight permanent; in short, how the thousands of episodes and events in a single life, my life, hold together.

Challenge of Modern Education

It is in the midst of these kinds of questions that contemporary educators must do their work. In the range and variety of formulations, education and academic inquiry must cut into the daily lives, the predicament, the yearning, that lie close to the root of our being.

The challenge of contemporary education is not so much a matter of discovering what we do not yet know. It is, instead, having the courage to say plainly what we really do know. It is time for us to make clear that those who characterize the big questions of truth, meaning, beauty, and goodness as being vague and unknowable are wrong.

Indeed, after several thousand years of inquiry, we have learned a great deal about the difference between the trivial and the profound, and the difference between the humane and the inhumane, and we have learned much about what things debase and what things ennoble human existence.

We know, too, that there are unavoidable experiences in human life shared by all persons, experiences that professors and students hold in common. These unavoidable conditions—birth, sexuality, promising, lying, forgiving, remembering, dreaming, dying—are all as provocative as they are mysterious. It is these aspects of life that have led to the configurations of writing, speaking, drawing, singing, counting, remembering, praying, and acting that have become the content of our academic courses. And they are also what we all are *always* in the process of experiencing and rationalizing.

Teaching about and inquiring into these things—things we know not as information but as meaning—ultimately is a matter of priorities and values, not of technique. This is because if our own insights are truly known and understood, they cut deeply into our lives—which is, after all, the heart of the matter. The end of knowledge is not the accumulation of bits of information, however interesting they may be. It is always, finally, the focusing of what we know on the living of our lives, and on having the courage to live in light of our deepened awareness.

Working as if the Earth Is at Stake

Certainly we are infinitely fascinated with the prospect of fixing the giant bureaucratic machine that is displayed in higher education. It is a gargantuan task, perhaps impossible. There is no single formula, no intricate combination of resources, that will do the trick.

The professional issues are ones that we can and will solve—one way or another—if for no other reason than the majority of our colleagues will spend a great deal of time solving them. Let us devote reasonable attention to such issues.

But our prior obligation, one that is in accord with our cultural and professional responsibility, is to turn education around through an immediacy of thought and action that embodies what we claim are really the purposes of teaching and research.

We must now work, in other words, as if our lives and our Earth are at stake. Thirty or forty years ago R. D. Laing wrote:

What we think is less than what we know; what we know is less than what we love; and what we love is so much less than what there is. And to that precise extent, we are so much less than what we are.

To work at the intersections of love, knowledge, and being—to work not just in our heads but in the world—will require a radical shift in the architecture of knowledge, so that it more clearly resembles the architecture of the human spirit.

Putting New Bite into Knowledge
Gustavo López Ospina

For UNESCO as well as for the international community this meeting comes at the right time. We are in the process of reflection, seeking new ideas and trying to arrive at concrete criteria to promote sustainable development worldwide. This is a very big challenge, not only for the North but also for the South, for both the industrialized and the developing countries. We are in a period of transition, characterized by much confusion in terms of content and often in terms of visions and policies from one country to another.

Before I go further, though, on behalf of our Director General, Mr. Federico Mayor, I want to thank the World Bank for inviting UNESCO to cosponsor this workshop. This is a very important marriage of effort between the Bank and UNESCO. Finance, knowledge, intelligence, and solidarity are critical yet very explosive and very sensitive interrelated issues.

International Initiatives

In setting the agenda for our discussions, I would like to mention some current activities at the international level in the field of education that may be helpful in this vulnerable time.

A great deal is being done in the context of the UN Commission for Sustainable Development. UNESCO is very much involved with this work in its function as task manager for the implementation of chapter 36 of Agenda 21 that addresses education, public awareness, and training. In 1996, the commission decided to give special priority to chapter 36 by adopting a special work program intended to galvanize and orient action at international and national levels. Another important stream of work relates to implementing the action plan of the Cairo conference on population, as well as the action plans of the other United Nations conferences such as the Social Summit in Copenhagen, the women's conference in Beijing, and Habitat II.

Just after the important World Bank meeting on knowledge held in Toronto, a special session of the United Nations General Assembly was held to review progress since the Earth Summit. The General Assembly adopted a resolution that referred to education as follows: "A fundamental prerequisite for sustainable development is an adequately financed and effective educational system at all levels." In describing effective education for sustainability, the resolution refers to lifelong learning, interdisciplinary studies, partnerships, multicultural education, and empowerment. Education for a sustainable future should, the resolution said, engage a wide spectrum of institutions and sectors, including business, industry, international organizations, youth, professional organizations, nongovernmental organizations, higher education, government, educators, and foundations. Finally, the resolution requests that the concept of education for a sustainable future be fully developed by UNESCO, in cooperation with other partners in the UN system and others in the international and scientific communities. It also notes that "it is necessary to support and strengthen universities and other academic centres."

To further these goals, in October, 1998, UNESCO will hold a major World Conference on Higher Education in Paris. In preparing this conference, regional meetings on higher education have been held throughout the world. In addition, we are holding a world conference on science in 1999. Other initiatives of relevance to our discussions are the reports of the International Commission on Education for the Twenty-first Century and that of a similar independent commission on culture and development, both published last year.

Education for Sustainable Development

I would now like to introduce a few elements that I hope will assist our collective thinking about organizing knowledge for environmentally sustainable development.

Humanity takes many years, sometimes hundreds of years, to develop and adopt very important concepts and definitions such as love, justice, and divorce. Today we are attempting to develop in just a few years and at a global scale a new way of thinking about and managing human activity and its impact on natural systems. I believe sustainable development is possible. I also believe that such profound change cannot be achieved without giving priority attention to the role of knowledge and education. This having been said, there is much confusion and disagreement about what is meant by the still-evolving concept of sustainable development.

Let us begin at the beginning. We cannot talk about education for sustainability without first addressing the challenge of education for all. This is the challenge that UNESCO and its partners—UNICEF, United Nations Development Programme (UNDP), and the World Bank—took up at the World Conference on Education for All, in Jomtien, in 1990, where the international community committed itself to a program of action for meeting basic learning needs, reducing illiteracy, expanding social services for children, and improving the quality of vocational education.

The other fundamental aspect of education—the prerequisite for all forms of educational advance—is lifelong education. The concept of "throughout life" is the most important addition recently made to educational thinking. Education must no longer be regarded as a one-chance affair, restricted to a particular period of a person's life. It must be seen—at all levels—as a continuing process, whereby people are offered learning opportunities throughout their lives by means of diversified delivery systems, both formal and informal.

Most people agree that a more educated society is, by definition, a more developed society. At the same time it is also necessary for our purposes to view education, even in developed societies, as a process of changing values and lifestyles, disseminating existing knowledge about the need to achieve sustainable production and to improve the management of natural resources, and promoting a willingness within the general population to accept the changes required. In many countries, it is the people themselves in the end who will decide what they want and need, both in the present and for the future. They will also decide how they will meet these needs. For determining new directions and new horizons, knowledge is indispensable for any society. Similarly, knowledge is the most important asset of citizens in a genuine democracy: I participate, therefore I exist.

In this context, the goals of education for sustainable development can be summarized as follows:
- To promote understanding of the interdependence of natural, socioeconomic, and political systems at local, national, and global levels
- To encourage critical reflection and decision-making that is reflected in personal lifestyles
- To engage the active participation of the citizenry to building sustainable development
- To promote effective governance at all levels.

An International "Democracy of Knowledge"

I would like to present for your consideration four key questions that I think should be at the heart of our debate, all of which are based on the premise that it is knowledge that will provide the fuel for change toward sustainable development. These four questions are:
  1. What kind of knowledge is needed to support sustainable development?

2. How can we obtain this knowledge?
3. What is the situation with regard to this knowledge today?
4. What are the necessary steps for us to move into the future?

What is needed is interdisciplinary knowledge that provides a basis for understanding and solving highly complex, real world problems at national, regional, and local levels. Such knowledge is not as theoretical as it may sound, or an objective in itself, but rather an approach to action. Achieving such knowledge and understanding requires the breaking down of traditional disciplinary boundaries and the creation of a new capability to address the profound questions posed by the notion of sustainability. In general we must strive for a new degree of knowledge integration that will mirror current economic, social, political, ecological, and technological realities, as well as the diverse requirements of human society, and indeed, of life itself.

As a step toward such integration, we must reinvent the universities of today so that they can contribute to what I would call an "international democracy of knowledge," that will help move the world toward a sustainable future without losing regional identities and the diversity of cultures. The challenge, as identified in chapter 36 of Agenda 21, is no less than that of reorienting education toward sustainable development. To do so will require a transdisciplinary approach that highlights the interrelationships between disciplines and allows for study and research across the traditional disciplinary lines.

In this process the trend toward cultural homogenization needs to be overcome. All too often because of this tendency, particularly in the developing countries, people find that the information they have is not what they want, the information they want is not what they need, and the information they need is not what they can obtain. Reversing this paradoxical, unhelpful situation is what I mean by an international democracy of knowledge.

Modern science, for example, is increasingly recognizing the value of indigenous ecological knowledge and traditional resource management practices based on generations of observation, experimentation, and application in local cultures, although globalization is posing a serious threat to such diversity. As a result, peoples and cultures that have existed for thousands of years in equilibrium with the natural environment are disappearing along with the ecosystems that sustained them.

At present, however, there is a very serious gap between the availability of scientific knowledge and its effective use as a basis for decision-making and education, including use by the media.

Risk and Imagination

Another key notion is that of risk, which is a necessary part of innovation and change. Risk without knowledge is dangerous, and knowledge without risk is utopian. Here again, knowledge must be *out there* in the real world, where it can serve humanity in solving the problems we face. The academic community has a dual responsibility in this regard, to make available the wealth of knowledge in its possession, and to make the strategic link between this knowledge and the key sectors driving political, economic, and social change. Knowledge, the driving force of modern society, should set the course of action in each of these sectors.

Another important notion is that of imagination. During periods of real crisis, conflict, and confusion, such as the present, imagination can actually be equally important as, or even more important than, knowledge. If we accept this premise, we need to recognize the urgent need to shape and communicate a new vision for the future and to anticipate, challenge, and create opportunities for positive change in social, scientific, cultural, economic, and natural spheres. At all levels of society, people need security, motivation, hope, and a sense of choice. Meeting these human needs is never an easy task, but with imagination it is possible to look beyond the present period of transition to conceive of a sustainable future based on what people want and need.

How is knowledge necessary for people to transform their future? Part of the answer lies in the issue of how to connect universities with the scientific system, and from this link to create and offer an understanding, a language, an articulation of values that will be heard in the productive sector. Today we have new ways to help build this link, to organize the academic and scientific communities to provide information resources in different issues such as agriculture and industry, making it possible from that point to address specific details of these issues. We also have other important centers that can be helpful. In short, we have at our disposal facilities from the national to the global scale with which to create and provide new knowledge for sustainability.

What are the key challenges in the introduction and application of such knowledge? One is how to ensure the appropriateness of this knowledge for societies' needs. A related challenge is how to provide access to this knowledge at the community level in order to allow for real participation in natural resources management and utilize the understanding gained from this participation to help address the tremendous complexities inherent in these issues. However difficult, I am convinced that it can be done.

Another challenge is how to give real priority to this newly achieved popular knowledge to produce a new societal rationale. There is a great need at present for a global ethic, transcending all other systems of values and belief, rooted in a consensus of the relatedness and the sanctity of all life. However, as Socrates said, it may be easy to know what is or is not correct, but it is often very difficult to know what is right in terms of action.

In concluding, let me also introduce an important political issue at the international level. We may believe that knowledge, equity, and justice are key ingredients for a sustainable future, but also, at the community level, we need concurrently to reinforce the ideas of solidarity and competitiveness. Here the university and all the institutions of higher education have, today and into the next century, a four-part key responsibility:

- Knowledge-building for the real and concrete world problems
- Democratization of knowledge at all levels of society
- Knowledge base for global understanding, solidarity, justice, and peace
- Knowledge for a permanent transformation and reinvention of education as a principal instrument to support a sustainable future.

This is the only way to alleviate poverty, to achieve a new human security and cohesiveness, and to work for a real culture of peace.

Shifting Gears for the Application of Knowledge

Don Aitkin

My topic is a straightforward one. It regards the need to think about how we generate knowledge in the interests of a world in which that knowledge is desperately needed.

I can set out the problem clearly enough—it is that we remain in the grip of an old paradigm about the creation of knowledge, one that was useful in its day but is almost counterproductive now. It is hard to get out of the grip of this paradigm because it seems so much to be the normal way of doing things, especially in the universities and the learned professions.

I will make some suggestions about what we should do to escape this situation, and I know that these suggestions will be resisted and opposed, because I have made them before, and that is what happened then. The need is great, however, so I will make them again.

Linear Model of Knowledge

In fact the old paradigm is not very old. Nothing much in the higher education world is really very old; it is mostly the creation of the nineteenth and twentieth centuries, despite the way that we refer to the universities as having outlived everything but the Catholic Church.

The current way of thinking got a great boost at the end of the Second World War when Vannevar Bush successfully advised President Harry S Truman that he should establish a National Science Foundation (NSF), so that science could flourish and the United States could, in effect, win the peace as it had won the war—through science.

Vannevar Bush was especially clear about one central aspect of his proposal: scientists should be allowed to follow their own noses in determining what research should be done.

He was a great believer in what we would now call the linear model of knowledge: that is, that pure, untrammeled research leads to discoveries about the nature of things that in turn leads to the application of new knowledge, and, in the fullness of time, leads to new products and new processes through commercialization and development.

The causal arrow is a straight one and there are no feedback loops. The notion that scientists should not only be allowed to follow their own noses, but should be given public money to do so has been understandably attractive to scientists. Because during that post-war period many of them worked in universities, access to research funds on what proved to be a large scale helped in the expansion of the universities and made the carrying out of research, in some form, an ordinary expectation of academic life, that it had not been prior to the Second World War.

Since the NSF model was adopted by several other Western countries in whole or in part, the consequence has been a great increase in research activity throughout the Western world. This whole process was greatly assisted by other stimuli, the most important of them being sustained prosperity for three decades; a new interest in education, especially higher education; and the growth of an academic profession whose members assume that they are not simply to teach, but also to carry out research.

One outcome has been a very great increase in the amount of what we call human knowledge, that is perhaps better defined as "what academics think they know." It is hard to measure this increase accurately, but it has been something in the order of 30 to 50 times what was known around 1950.

For instance, there are now more than half a million scholarly journals in the world, and libraries that once aimed at comprehensiveness, such as the Library of Congress or the Bodleian at Oxford, are no longer able to do so.

In fact every library, every person, and every institution now has to be selective. Advanced information technology has come at just at the right time, enabling us to select what we want to know from the mad abundance of knowledge that is available. By the way, there is much more noise than there is knowledge. The information technology brings its own problems with it, although I am not going to talk about that now. The subject is for another address at some other conference.

The great increase in knowledge has come with two very powerful concurrent effects. The first has been the continuing atomization of knowledge, with a consequent kind of elephantiasis in the old scholarly disciplines. Elephantiasis is indeed a very painful disease.

Decline of the Generalists

Johann von Goethe and John Stuart Mill in the early nineteenth century have been credited as the last people who knew everything there was to be known. Today, it is not even possible to know everything in one scholarly discipline. Everyone is a specialist, and generalists are held in some suspicion, if not in outright scorn.

Before the Second World War it was possible to be somebody called a social scientist, or to be called a scientist, expert in one field but knowledgeable across them all. One celebrated man of my own country held chairs at different times in philosophy, political science, sociology, and education, and he published in all of these areas, and well. I cannot think of a single counterpart today.

When I was a young academic in the early 1960s there were several broad divisions within my own discipline, and you were expected to become knowledgeable in one but to have at least a passing knowledge of the names and the issues in the others.

Accomplishing such breadth would be a Herculean task today, and the specialties that academics now profess seem, historically, very narrow in comparison.

There is a good reason for this change in academic perspective and it is one that I discovered only quite recently. An intellectual program, that is, a group of people focused on a question that interests them all and that they think is important, does not work if the group of people is much more than five hundred. Once the numbers become much greater, the question breaks into an adjectival or otherwise qualified version of the original question, and you have two groups. It is a kind of cellular fission.

True, knowledge has expanded, but not through leaps of insight and the discovery of the general rules underlying adjoining broad fields of study that was one of the great dreams when I was young. The expansion has been mostly through incremental additions to what is already known.

It is also true that the boundaries between research areas have been fertile ground for new research, but this, in turn, has been followed by the erection of new boundaries, and the naming of new specialties. Review articles aside, published research is, for the most part, restricted to the small, the narrow gauge, and the incremental.

Few researchers are brave enough to generalize, and they always need to duck the sniping fire of the specialists. There is much more that could be said here, notably about the part played by journals and the institution of the Ph.D. as the certification of the learned that has fueled much of the production of knowledge, and about the way in which disciplinary knowledge has become territory, defended against other disciplines and the undisciplined alike. This, too, is for another address at another conference.

A Shift in the Universities

The second major concurrence of the increase in knowledge has been the elevation of research to its dominant place in the world of higher education, and the shift of universities toward being suppliers of new knowledge rather than hosts of teaching and of learning.

The linear model that I talked about earlier has given universities a special place in the generation of knowledge, because it is the universities that particularly concentrate on pure research, which is thought to be the foundation of all knowledge.

Interestingly, the research university is actually quite a recent phenomenon in the nearly 1,000-year history of institutions of higher education. Indeed until our own century it would be easy to show that advances in knowledge came more from outside the university than that from inside it.

Now let me move from the old paradigm about which I have said enough to the modern problem. In this regard, we live in a world of 6 billion human beings who, if nothing else changes, will number 12 billion by the middle of the next century.

Through our sheer abundance as a species we already put tremendous pressure on our planet. Most of us now live in cities of one kind or another, and the urban proportion of humanity's activity is rising steadily.

Our cities cover great areas; create huge demands for food and fresh water; require complex communications, transport, sewerage, education, and civil order systems; and create dreadful environments in terms of water, air, and soil pollution, not to mention the potential for epidemic disease, developed among undernourished urban populations through viral and respiratory pathogens. The problem is us.

Whatever the solutions are—and I want to suggest some—they need to be general or holistic. Just as a wise physician treats his patient, not the disease that is the symptom of some underlying cause, so in building a sustainable world in which human beings can thrive, we need to see our major policies as being at the broad level of the societies in which human beings live.

This holistic approach puts a different demand on knowledge because, as I have noted, human knowledge now advances increment by tiny increment; the guardians of the increments are specialists who are often unable to link what they know to what other specialists know.

Meanwhile, pure understanding of the highly dynamic contemporary social processes is a long way off, while the need for quick action has been clear for many years.

A Strategy Regarding Knowledge

There would seem to be a way out of this dilemma. To begin with, we can realize that it is not necessary to think that we must always search for new knowledge, especially when we frequently cannot wait for it to be generated. We already know a great deal about our predicament and it can make sense to employ, first of all, this knowledge that we already possess. I would like to give two examples.

The first example is the growing discovery throughout the nineteenth century of the linked importance of clean water, sanitation, hygienic practices, and fresh air in reducing mortality and morbidity in the urban populations of Europe and America.

What we now regard as the ordinary municipal services or public utilities needed for any human settlement other than that of a tiny size grew out of that nineteenth century experience in Western countries.

There have been at least 100 years of acceptance of this need in our developed world, to the point that our contemporary city populations probably cannot imagine that it was ever thought otherwise.

In the rapidly expanding cities of the developing world, there is neither similar understanding of such need nor experience with our solutions. What the situation calls for is not ever ingenious remedies to particular diseases, but major preventative measures that deal with these diseases at the root by avoiding them in the first place.

In this case we already have the knowledge that is necessary for the people of these cities. It is not dramatic, or new, or a breakthrough. It is old-fashioned and it still works.

The second example is the link between smoking tobacco and the onset of lung cancer and other diseases such as emphysema, a link that has been well known for two generations. The move to discourage smoking was slow to occur because people who smoke like to smoke and find it hard to give up the practice even when they want to, and also because growing tobacco is a virtuous farming activity and making cigarettes is an industry that employs people. Governments, that also obtain revenue through taxing tobacco products, engage in the discouragement of smoking diffidently.

What the governments finally did was to draw people's attention to the fact that smoking is bad for the health, and compelling the manufacturers of tobacco products to print warnings on the packets.

In time nonsmokers and ex-smokers began to complain of the risk they ran of disease contracted through other people's smoking, and the practice began to be discouraged or even banned in workplaces, public buildings, restaurants, and airplanes.

The outcome of this story, that continues today, has been a great reduction in the incidence of lung cancer and related disease on the part of those who have stopped smoking. Of course it does continue as a practice and it is still seen by some young people as glamorous and adult. Overall, though, the reduction in healthcare costs has been enormous.

Once again this advance has not come through a breakthrough in research. If you get lung cancer the treatment of choice is still the one used 30 years ago. There has been no great breakthrough in how to treat lung cancer, but there has been an enormous breakthrough in how to prevent people from getting it in the first place, and it is that kind of mission that I suggest is the crucial one.

Key Role of Education

The smoking reduction effort has worked partly because governments have had the resolve to keep up their advocacy despite the intense objection to it from pro-smoking interests, and because our populations are sufficiently well-educated to be able to make up their own minds.

This education factor points to another of the great levers available to us in contemplating the world of the future. We need to always be aware that a well-educated population can do a great deal through understanding its own dilemma and taking appropriate action to combat it.

If I combine the lessons from the urban service and smoking reduction examples, I get the possibility of a strategy, which is: Use the knowledge we already have and tell people what is known.

Reflecting on my point just a moment ago, there may be a third element to the strategy: Put as much effort into education as possible, because the better educated people are, the more they are likely to take responsibility for their own welfare. Perhaps there is a fourth element: Ensure that governments or national agencies have the knowledge and the support to undertake the first three elements of the strategy.

My own view is that these precepts provide all that is necessary for a well-intentioned national government and that international funding agencies need little more than the combination of these precepts plus a well-intentioned government.

This seems so easy that of course we might say it must be unworkable. What may be a worry is that the strategy runs counter to the prevailing orthodoxy that government intervention to produce outcomes is usually wrong, always productive of unintended consequences, never as beneficial as letting the market solve the problem.

It is because my own principal background has been in history and political science rather than in economics that I am not a great believer in the creative capacity of markets to transform human societies. In any case much of what I have been describing as humanity's problem can be explained in economics under the rubric of market failure.

Links among Governments and Universities

If such a conclusion is allowed, let us move to the third section of this paper which offers some suggestions about what might be done in the knowledge industry.

To start, I want to dispose of any suggestion that I favor getting rid of pure research or having all research targeted or applied. This is not my view. Human curiosity is a powerful weapon in the advancement of knowledge, and Vannevar Bush was right to think that the intellectual curiosity of researchers themselves will probably get them further than following the mundane priorities of other people.

There are other useful human qualities apart from curiosity, and compassion and problem-solving are two others that can work very well in dealing with human predicaments.

What we need and what in fact we do not have—and here is a connection with Dr. Ladner's paper—is an easy linkage between governments and universities in the area of knowledge application.

Some of the reasons for this lack of connection are financial. Our governments are now chronically short of money and unable or unwilling to raise more through increased taxation.

Some of the reasons are functions of scale. There is so much knowledge available, but often so little agreement about what is relevant to a given problem.

Some reasons are cultural. Governments and universities have different senses of time, different meanings for the word "deadline," and different imperatives.

Some reasons are territorial. Universities see knowledge as their own product and want to surround it with various rules, while governments and funding agencies are uninterested in ownership and recognize that knowledge always has to be applied in a real and dirty world, not in an aseptic laboratory or through a computer model.

Other reasons are epistemological. A lot of knowledge is conjectural rather than factual, and governments are reluctant outside the area of economics to rely too much on theories and possibilities. They want certainty and do not understand the universities' needs for extensive and continuing critique.

What is more—and this is really fundamental—Western governments seem to have lost confidence in their capacity to achieve good outcomes through social and economic policy. This makes them especially leery of pinning their faith on the outcomes of research in universities.

Thirty years ago things in this regard were different. There was a prevailing belief that, in principle at least, all human problems—whether social, economic, or political—were solvable, provided there was sufficient knowledge, money,

and will. Quite apart from the financial question, we do not think this way any longer. The more we know, the harder it all seems.

Principles and Policies

We turn now to my suggestions. I have to say at once that there is not much use directing suggestions like this at universities, though I do so, because universities have a strong sense of their own virtue and are inclined to see the responsibility lying elsewhere.

I direct these thoughts mostly at governments and international funding agencies, because they have some capacity, through their actions, to change thinking inside universities, and universities have become very, very large parts of the society in the industrial world.

The first of my suggestions is this: we need to recognize that in dealing with large human populations the policy prescriptions must be simple, they must be easy to explain, and they must be based on past success somewhere. Developing such policies requires, among other things, the use of historically knowledgeable generalists, which good historians often are.

The second suggestion is to recognize that we already know a lot, and we should be prepared to distill that knowledge in a form that allows it to be transferred to new situations. Things that work in one country may not work in another, for straightforward reasons of history, culture, or level of technology.

Knowing when, and when not, to try to transfer policy successes will require, among other things, the use of generalists who find it easy to compare, enjoy doing so, and are good at it.

Third, when in doubt, governments and funding agencies should prefer the long term, though balancing the long term with the short term is the hardest part of policymaking. The long-term goal is a sustainable world, and the aim should be to empower populations to make good decisions for themselves, rather than having to rely on others to decide for them.

Even good short-term policies should have excellent long-term outcomes. For example, equipping shantytown dwellers with decent housing, running water, electricity, and sewerage will not only improve their material conditions, but will give them a stake in the preservation of the society that they live in.

These first few suggestions are not at all radical, and indeed they are almost banal. They point to a mismatch with what governments and funding agencies are typically involved in the world of the university, because these suggestions do not require or depend on much new research.

Somehow we need to develop many people who are capable of interpreting research findings in one field and linking them to those in other fields, so that the joint use of this knowledge is possible.

This does not mean that we should flood the world with historians: many of them are specialists too. What it does mean is that in seeking to use the knowledge that universities have developed in the last half century, we need to start by making clear what results we are seeking, and then attract people who find the challenge of applying existing knowledge to produce a given outcome to be an interesting one.

Points on Funding Research

I finish with three quite pointed suggestions about the funding of research on the part of governments and international funding agencies.

1. Encourage applications and resist the cry that understanding must come first. As Benjamin Ladner said, we do not ordinarily devote ourselves to complete understanding before we do things anyway. Life is short and the tasks are many.

2. Encourage outcome-oriented social science. Attract the best practitioners to work not on models and theories, but on the real world in all its difficulty and noise.

3. Encourage cross-disciplinary work. The disciplines of the university are divisions of academic history and convenience, and they get in the way of real world analysis. They cannot be ignored, however, because the very knowledge that we talk about is largely organized within disciplinary boundaries. The solution is to make sure that projects are based on cross-disciplinary teams that comprise knowledgeable specialists.

While these several suggestions are hardly revolutionary, they do imply a shift in perspective from the generation of knowledge for its own sake to the generation of knowledge in the interests of humankind.

It is not at all difficult to justify such a shift. The problems facing us are large and daunting and the speed of change is very great. Surely that ought to be enough. In fact I do not think it is, and that is why I have made my suggestions to those who actually provide money to support the generation of knowledge. Academics in universities, as is the case with virtually all actors in modern, Western societies, are quite responsive to financial incentives. Quite small amounts of money, intelligently applied, can have powerful cultural effects.

Shifting Requirements for Knowledge to Advance a Sustainable South

Partha Dasgupta

The Resource Basis of Human Well-Being and Its Neglect

People in poor countries are for the most part agrarian and pastoral. In 1988 rural people accounted for about 65 percent of the population of what the World Bank classifies as low-income countries. The proportion of the total labor force in agriculture was a bit in excess of 65 percent. The share of agriculture in gross domestic product in these countries was 30 percent. These figures should be contrasted with those from industrial market economies, which are 6 percent and 2 percent for the latter two ratios respectively.

Rural communities in poor countries are bio-mass-based subsistence economies, in that poor people eke out a living from products obtained directly from plants and animals. For example, studies in the Indian subcontinent have shown that as much as 40 to 50 percent of the working hours of villagers are devoted to fodder and fuel collection, animal care, and grazing. Moreover inquiries in Central and West Africa have revealed the importance of forest products in rural people's lives. Poor countries, especially those in the Indian subcontinent and Sub-Saharan Africa, can be expected to remain largely rural economies for some while yet.

The dependence of poor countries on their natural resources such as soil and its cover, water, forests and their products, animals, and fisher-ies should be self-evident: Ignore the environmental resource base and we are bound to obtain a misleading picture of production and consumption activities there. Nevertheless, if there has been a single thread running through nearly fifty years of investigation into the poverty of poor countries, it has been a neglect of this resource base. Until very recently, environmental resources made but perfunctory appearances in government planning models and were cheerfully ignored in most of what goes by the name "development economics."

There were exceptions, of course. What I am referring to here is a neglect of environmental matters in what we could call official development economics. Thus, for example, the 1986 World Congress of the International Economic Association, held in New Delhi, had as its theme the appropriate balance between industry and agriculture. In the 16 sessions that comprised the congress, none was devoted to the environmental resource basis of production and consumption.

Handbooks offer another kind of illustration, reflecting as they do the attention researchers have given to various fields of inquiry. To me it is a revealing fact that the 2-volume *Handbook of Development Economics*, edited by Hollis Chenery and T. N. Srinivasan (1988) contains nothing on environmental matters. The environment appears in official development economics in much the same way as that most famous bark does in literature: it does not.

In a similar vein environmental and resource economics has neglected issues concerning rural poverty in poor countries. Thus the 3-volume *Handbook of Natural Resource and Energy Economics*, edited by Allen Kneese and James Sweeney (1985, 1993) contains nothing on poverty and its possible links with environmental degradation. Development and environmental economics have until recently passed each other by, and it is interesting to speculate why.

A prime reason often aired is that environmental and resource economists in Western industrial countries (especially the United States) have tended to focus on such problems as local air pollution, including sulfur emissions, and deterioration of amenities, including national parks, beaches, and coastlines.[1] To the development economist, environmental matters have appeared a trifle precious, not wholly relevant to the urgencies of poor countries. On innumerable occasions I have had this explanation offered to me by social scientists in poor countries. I would not wish to doubt it, but the explanation does not tell us why, when they studied development problems, these same social scientists ignored their own environmental resource base.

At an academic level the lack of contact between development and environmental economics has been harmful to both. Specialized fields are often driven by internal logic, and the gap between topics that are most intensively discussed and those that are most urgent and at once tractable can become large. As it happens, there was an additional loss due to the unwillingness of development and environmental economists to talk to one another. The economics of the environment, heavily involved as it is with the science of ecology, is an exciting subject. It is also a beautiful subject: there is much in it to enthuse young people.

There have been exceptions, of course. Over the years a number of social scientists have developed environmental and resource economics within the context of rural populations in poor countries. We now have in hand a body of work that studies the links between rural poverty, population growth, and the environmental resource base. The work has involved a fusion of theoretical modeling to empirical findings drawn from a number of disciplines, most notably anthropology, demography, ecology, economics,

geography, and political science. It offers a new perspective on economic development.[2] In recent years the twin subjects, resource economics and environmental economics, have together been labeled ecological economics. In the remainder of the article, I will follow this practice.

The foregoing remarks have stressed developments in the supply of ideas. There have also been changes in demand. As regards timing, the shift in attitude can probably be identified with the publication of the "Brundtland Report" (World Commission 1987); today no account of economic development would be regarded as adequate, even by economists in poor countries, if the environmental resource base were absent from it. The World Bank's excellent *World Development Report 1992* is an affirmation of this changed viewpoint.

This new awareness, on its own, will not be enough. Until the environmental resource base becomes a commonplace furniture of economic thinking and modeling in poor countries, it will continue to be neglected in the design and implementation of public policies there. Even if these policies are implemented, there is the danger that they will be reached through ad hoc measures. Moreover, teachers, researchers, and policymakers will remain oblivious of the tools that are available for the analysis of social and economic problems. They will remain unaware of the need for scientific information on the processes and functions of local ecological systems, and they will not recognize an allied point: There is an urgent need for poor countries to encourage the development of information channels that are conducive to good governance.

It is imperative that tomorrow's leaders in poor countries are not only more sensitive to the ecological concerns among their own citizens, but that they are also able to think on such concerns in a natural, unforced, and effective way. Tomorrow's decisionmakers are today's students. If ecological concerns are to become an essential part of economic thinking in poor countries, ecological economics has to enter university teaching there. In order for this to happen, however, university teachers of economics at those universities need to learn the subject. This thought has been the basis of a "Programme of Teaching and Research in Developing Countries" that I have helped initiate at the Beijer International Institute of Ecological Economics of the Royal Swedish Academy of Sciences, Stockholm, in collaboration with the institute's director, Professor Karl-Göran Mäler. In the following section I will describe this program (the Programme). In section III I will draw lessons from it, and in section IV I will suggest what the lessons seem to indicate as regards future capacity building in ecological economics in poor countries.

The Beijer Teaching and Research Programme in Poor Countries

The Programme's first component consists of teaching workshops for university teachers of economics. At each workshop, about 20 to 25 participants from poor countries attend a specially designed course on ecological economics. In order to save on airfares, the workshops are held regionally, with each workshop lasting 10 to 12 days. Participants and program staff live and eat together in the same hotel complex.[3] This means that intellectual and social interactions occur from breakfast through late evening every day. This interaction has been vital to the Programme's success. All expenses are borne by the Beijer Institute. It is our hope that over the next two years or so, about 150 university teachers of economics in poor countries will have attended these workshops.

Given that there are no suitable textbooks on ecological economics for use in poor countries, we have had to develop the syllabus ourselves. The reading list (and the lecture course) includes articles and book-chapters that offer basic ecology and advanced economic analysis. We spend about three days on these two subjects before entering the meat of the subject—ecological economics in the development context (see sections III and IV).

To date we have conducted five teaching workshops: one in Chile (for participants from South America), one in Jamaica (for participants from the Caribbean and Central America), one in Malaysia (for participants from Southeast Asia and Bangladesh), one in Malta (for participants from Sub-Saharan Africa), and one in Sri Lanka (for participants from parts of Sub-Saharan Africa and the Indian subcontinent). In short, the network we have created now includes about 120 university teachers from poor countries. They are linked to the Beijer Institute, the World Bank, and the Harvard Institute for International Development (HIID). This particular set of links has arisen because our "permanent" teaching staff are associated with these institutions. The Programme could not have been launched and sustained but for collegial friendship: there are little to no financial rewards for the Programme's teaching staff!

However, teaching workshops, on their own, would not be enough. At a minimum they need to be supplemented by such means as would enable ecological economists in poor countries to enter the international network of researchers. If, as we economists tend to believe, there are multiplier effects in the dissemination of knowledge, the eventual size of the network could be expected to be a good deal larger. The Beijer Programme's second component consists of research workshops at which participants from poor countries present their own research findings, works-in-progress, and research proposals in the presence of foreign peers. My hope is that through such workshops our colleagues in poor countries will enjoy the benefit of peer-group evaluation and criticism of the kind that we who are fortunate to work in advanced industrial countries take for granted. These workshops are also held regionally, and their expenses are borne by the Beijer Institute.

Who attends research workshops? To build a comprehensive educational program, we have pursued the following approach: we offer the research workshops as a carrot to those who have attended a teaching workshop. This way, those who have obtained training at the teaching workshops have an incentive not only to teach the subject to students in their own universities, but also to conduct research on their local environmental problems. We try to hold a research workshop about a year after a teaching workshop, and we invite previous participants to submit research papers to such workshops. To date, we have held four research workshops: in Malaysia, Malta, Tanzania, and Venezuela.

In addition we will be using some of the grant money to allow authors of the most promising submissions to a newly established journal (see immediately below) to improve them on the basis of visits to the relevant institutions (for example the World Bank, Beijer Institute, or HIID).

Mäler and I felt from the start that even this would not be enough. If capacity is to be built in poor countries in the field of ecological economics, teaching and research workshops need to be supplemented by the creation of opportunities for indigenous scholars to publish their work in reputable international journals. The establishment of a quarterly journal, *Environment and Development Economics* (EDE), published by Cambridge University Press, has been aimed at meeting this need. The first issue was out in February 1997; it forms the third component of the Beijer Programme.

The goal in starting the journal was to create a space where ecological and development economists from all parts of the world can publish their work. It is the intention of the editorial board to treat submissions from poor countries with the same care, sympathy, and critical standard that those scholars who work in the West take for granted. One way we are trying to ensure that submissions from poor countries meet the test of quality is to have policy forums, where authors can report and comment on environmental debates and discussions currently being undertaken in their own countries. Economists in poor countries constantly hear about global warming; it would be good if economists in the West were able to learn of the myriad of local environmental problems many in poor countries routinely face.

Intellectual infrastructure differs greatly within poor countries. Libraries in some universities subscribe to a wide range of international journals, whereas many others have an extreme paucity of subscriptions. Over an initial period of five years, the Beijer Institute is providing free subscriptions to EDE to libraries in the developing world recommended to us by participants of our teaching and research workshops. In addition, the grant money for the Beijer Programme is being used to supply, free of charge, a selection of books on ecological economics to the libraries of the institutions to which previous participants belong. The books in question form the basis of the teaching workshops.

Lessons

It will be apparent to the reader that the Beijer Programme I have described here is a multi-layered one: It locates young university professors of economics in poor countries (they are typically in their late twenties or early thirties) and offers them training, encouragement, guidance, and incentives to both teach ecological economics to their students, and to initiate research on their own.

Toward this end we have tried several methods to locate suitable candidates for participation. We have had help from such organizations as the Consortium of African Economists; we have had help from our own academic contacts in poor countries; we have advertised the workshops and solicited applications; we have written to department heads in more than 150 universities, asking them to nominate young colleagues; and we have sought the help of past participants in locating able colleagues who are interested in ecological economics. Selection has proved to be more difficult than we had originally thought (department heads are not often reliable, and often nominate themselves!), but we have learned quickly from experience.

As I mentioned earlier, the teaching staff for the Programme has been faithful to the cause because of friendship. We have a balanced staff, combining expertise in ecology, economic analysis, and applied environmental economics. (The participation of John Dixon of the World Bank has been particularly useful; the Bank has access to a large number of case studies that the Programme makes available to participants.) A typical teaching workshop of 20 participants and seven staff costs about US$120,000. Research workshops cost a bit less, because they are typically held over four to five days. Considering everything, this is an enormously productive investment. Even if the success rate eventually were to turn out to be as low as 10 percent—that is, even if only 10 percent of the participants in the teaching workshops were eventually to publish in EDE—it represents money well spent.

What have we learned from our experience?

1. As expected, talent and background expertise vary enormously across the continents. On average, participants from Sub-Saharan Africa had the weakest background, and those from Southeast Asia (Vietnam, for example) the best. Latin America is a lot more promising than I had

originally expected: there are plenty of good and concerned minds in Latin American universities.

2. There is enormous enthusiasm for the subject. Mäler and I had no idea that there is as much hunger for knowledge of economics in general, and for knowledge of ecological economics in particular, as we have observed among our young colleagues in poor countries. In short we do not have to sell ecological economics to university professors in poor countries: they want to learn it anyway. It is the opportunity they lack.

3. Our colleagues in poor countries have not as yet become dispirited about their own abilities. They still have ambition to teach new things and to publish the occasional article.

4. Our emphasis on teaching modern economic analysis to participants before getting down to details of social cost-benefit analysis has proved to be correct: participants have been particularly excited in seeing how even the most pedestrian problems about the environment are better informed when exposed to modern economic analysis. Mäler's (and my own) prejudice was that it would be a mistake to teach participants only the routine tools of ecological economics; we felt that the right way to go about things would be to create a syllabus that forces participants to become better economists before they launch themselves into ecological economics. This prejudice was entirely justified: most of our colleagues in poor countries lack a good grounding in modern economics. They know it; and they value most highly the fact that by the end of a teaching workshop they have seen how economic analysis can change their perception of how best to pose an environmental problem, let alone analyze it.

5. The learning curve is steep. It has been a particularly gratifying experience to observe, again and again, the difference in the ability of the average participant to discuss an environmental problem on the first days of a workshop and on the last day of the workshop.

The Future

What do these lessons indicate about future courses of action? Three recommendations suggest themselves: they involve the short run, the medium run, and the long run. I will consider them sequentially:

The Short Term

Of immediate concern is a request we have begun to receive from past participants. A number of them now want to prepare syllabi and reading lists for courses on ecological economics they wish to establish at their own universities. They have asked the Beijer Institute for help in devising the appropriate syllabi. Since the prime intent of the Programme was to have ecological economics taught in poor countries, we need to be able to provide this help. However, if we are to give this help, we need funds to enable members of our staff to visit such universities as those that seek help, spend a few days understanding the existing economics program, address seminars in the presence of their senior colleagues in order to legitimize the desire, and then advise our hosts on how best they could devise the syllabus. Fortunately, this involves small amounts of money. We could, for example, select a few key universities (totaling six to seven in number in Africa, Asia, and Latin America), and help create the teaching syllabus.

The Medium Term

To date the Beijer Programme has been supported by grants from the United Nations University's World Institute of Development Economics Research (UNU/WIDER), in 1992 and 1994; the Swedish International Development Authority (SIDA), in 1995; and, more recently (1995–98), from a block grant from the MacArthur Foundation.[4] The latter grant will enable us not only to organize several teaching and research workshops, but also to finance some of the expenses associated with our journal, and support the completion of research by some of the most promising submissions to the journal from poor countries. The MacArthur grant is being phased over four years. It started in 1995, it peaks in 1997, and trails off in 1998. If the Beijer Programme is to have a lasting impact, it needs to consolidate about 250 economists in poor countries into the network that we are creating. This means that it needs funding until the end of the century. This is something the SIDA may wish to consider, along with possibly assisting with support for the creation of the teaching syllabi.

The Long Term

The emergence of the Internet is going to prove tremendously important in enabling our colleagues in poor countries to join the international academic network. In the final analysis, however, nothing can replace personal contact. You really need to be in close association with colleagues in poor countries to realize how starved they are for the kind of collegial contact, encouragement, and help that makes academic life creative in the West. Many years ago the physicist Abdus Salam recognized the importance of this and created, with the help of UNESCO and the Italian government among other agencies, the International Centre for Theoretical Physics in Trieste. A number of physicist friends of mine working in poor countries have told me how important their visits to this institute have been in enabling them to "recharge" themselves intellectually during sabbaticals and vacations. Over the long run I am convinced we need to establish something like such an institute, but located in a university campus in a poor country with good infrastructure, such as Mauritius.

What I have in mind is an institute that would only have visitors and a minimum permanent staff. The institute's purpose would be to facilitate colleagues in poor countries in their desire to teach and conduct research at the interface of anthropology, ecology, economics, demography, geography, and political science, where the subject of ecological economics resides.[5] The institute could facilitate scholars' visits during their vacations and sabbaticals by offering financial aid. The institute would also invite internationally distinguished colleagues in these same fields to come on short-term visits to deliver lectures, conduct seminars, and interact with the institute's prime visitors. In other words the institute's mission would be to offer an intellectual haven for scholars from poor countries. Teaching and re-search workshops, such as those in the Beijer Programme, could also be located at the institute.

Professor Salam, I believe, had in mind that the International Centre for Theoretical Physics would be a place from which outstanding research in theoretical physics from poor countries would be generated. I do not know if he has been successful in this aim. My own belief is that, in my own field, we are some years away from the time when we can expect pioneering research to flow from universities in, say, Sub-Saharan Africa. I am not suggesting that establishing an institute of the kind I have sketched will produce high-quality research output from poor countries in the immediate future. Its mission would lie elsewhere. It would be a place where scholars would be able to rejuvenate themselves intellectually and keep somewhat abreast of contemporary ideas.

Vast sums are spent annually in the support of higher education in poor countries. Minor rechanneling of resources could greatly improve the performance of those who teach in these places. Capacity building involves a wide range of activities. The Beijer Programme that I have described in this article is a very small part of this. All my experience tells me now that it is a very important part. Fortunately it is, relatively speaking, an inexpensive part.

Notes

1. For confirmation see Cropper and Oates (1992), which reports almost exclusively on valuation techniques and cost-effective regulation of pollution.

2. See for example C.S.E. (1982, 1985), Dasgupta (1982, 1993, 1995), Anderson (1987), Agarwal and Narain (1989), Barrett (1989), Dixon, James, and Sherman (1989), Falconer and Amold (1989), Bojö, Mäler, and Unema (1990), Dixon, James, and Sherman (1990), Binswanger (1991), Dasgupta and Mäler (1991, 1995, 1996), Solorzano and others (1991), World Bank (1992), Dixon and others (1994), and Ehrlich, Ehrlich, and Daily (1995). I am stressing rural economies not because urban environmental problems do not exist in poor countries—they are rampant—but because the rural sector reveals novel character in the nature of environmental problems in poor countries.

3. It has been our policy to hold the workshops in isolated places, not in metropolitan centers, so that participants are not tempted to stray from the purpose at hand.

4. The grant from UNO/WIDER helped us prepare material that is of use in teaching ecological economics to people from poor countries.

5. See Dasgupta (1993).

References

Agarwal, A., and S. Narain. 1989. "Towards Green Villages: A Strategy for Environmentally Sound and Participatory Rural Development." Centre for Science and Environment, New Delhi.

Anderson, D. 1987. *The Economics of Afforestation.* Baltimore: The Johns Hopkins University Press.

Barrett, S. 1989. "Economic Growth and Environmental Conservation." London School of Economics. Ph.D. dissertation.

Binswanger, H. 1991. "Brazilian Policies That Encourage Deforestation in the Amazon." *World Development* 19.

Bojö, J., K.-G. Mäler, and L. Unema. 1990. *Environment and Development: An Economic Approach.* Amsterdam: Klewer.

Chenery, H., and T. N. Srinivasan. 1988. *Handbook of Development Economics.* Amsterdam: North Holland.

Cropper, M., and W. Oates. 1992. "Environmental Economics: A Survey." *Journal of Economic Literature* 30.

C. S. E. 1982, 1985. *The State of India's Environment: A Citizen's Report.* New Delhi: Centre for Science and Environment.

Dasgupta, P. 1982. *The Control of Resources.* Cambridge: Harvard University Press.

_____. 1993. *An Inquiry into Well-Being and Destitution.* Oxford: Clarendon Press.

_____. 1995. "The Population Problem: Theory and Evidence." *Journal of Economic Literature* 33.

Dasgupta, P., and K.-G. Mäler. 1991. "The Environment and Emerging Development Issues." *Proceedings of the World Bank Annual Conference on Development Economics 1990.* Washington, D.C.: World Bank.

_____. 1995. "Poverty, Institutions and the Environmental Resource-Base." In J. Behrman and T. N. Srinivasan, eds., *Handbook of Development Economics,* vol. IIIA. Amsterdam: North Holland.

_____, eds. 1996. *The Environment, Development, and Economic Analysis.* Oxford: Oxford University Press.

Dixon, J. A., D. E. James, and P. B. Sherman. 1989. *The Economics of Dryland Management.* London: Earthscan Publications.

_____, eds. 1990. *Dryland Management: Economic Case Studies.* London: Earthscan Publications.

Dixon, J. A., and others. 1994. *Economic Analysis of Environmental Impacts.* London: Earthscan Publications.

Ehrlich, P. R., A. H. Ehrlich, and G. C. Daily. 1995. *The Stork and the Plow: The Equity Answer to the Human Dilemma.* New York: G. P. Putnam's Sons.

Falconer, J., and J. E. M. Arnold. 1989. "Household Food Security and Forestry: An Analysis of Socio-Economic Issues." Food and Agriculture Organization of the United Nations, Rome.

Kneese, A., and J. Sweeney. 1985, 1993. *Handbook of Natural Resource and Energy Economics.* Amsterdam: North Holland.

Solorzano, R., and others. 1991. "Accounts Overdue: Natural Resource Depreciation in Costa Rica." World Resources Institute, Washington, D.C.

World Bank. 1992. *World Development Report 1992: Development and the Environment.* New York: Oxford University Press.

World Commission on Environment and Development. 1987. "Brundtland Report." New York: Oxford University Press.

_____. 1987. *Our Common Future.* New York: Oxford University Press.

Discussion

Tariq Husain: Let us open this session up for discussion. We will have questions from the audience for either Partha Dasgupta, Donald Aitkin, or Gustavo López Ospina, and then we will have our next speaker.

Audience comment: This is a comment on the various presentations that we heard today. I would like to mention one of the consequences of the development of knowledge that was somehow referred to but not directly. The development of knowledge creates ignorance, and this is a very important fact. It is not only a negative fact, it is also a positive fact, and I will try to explain this.

How can the development of knowledge create ignorance? Very simple. Our intellectual capacity is finite. Don Aitkin said that knowledge has developed to a much greater extent than our capacity. He said that Goethe and John Stuart Mill were the last people who could embrace all knowledge. This is not true. We have been unable to embrace all knowledge since ancient Greece, and the only people of whom we can say with more or less certainty that they did embrace all knowledge were the seven sages of ancient Greece. Nobody else since that time could embrace all knowledge.

What are the consequences of this? The fact that our individual knowledges are limited produces interdependence among humans, because we all become dependent on the knowledge that others have that we do not have. Interestingly enough, knowledge forces us to collaborate, and thus brings us together, all of our academic disciplines and differences notwithstanding.

Knowledge also brings us together for another reason: It creates threats for humanity through the development of technologies that can have adverse, sometimes disastrous effects. Four centuries ago, Francis Bacon said knowledge is power, and he overturned the age-old tradition of a distinction between pure and practical knowledge. In fact all knowledge is practical. All knowledge has consequences that go beyond the knower and transform the world and us within it.

The threats that we have created ourselves, through the development of knowledge, make us aware that we are in the same boat and must collaborate, and that we cannot live and behave as we have behaved in the past, disregarding the other person, other cultures, and other societies. We are therefore all interdependent in view of the threat that we have created to humanity, and this will have very far-reaching consequences for the development of humanity.

Audience comment: One of the major problems when we talk about knowledge with regard to the developing world, and here I refer to my own country, the Congo, is poverty. In order to share the knowledge, the rational knowledge that people gain from school, you need to have some financial possibilities. In most of these countries where people do not have sufficient income it is very difficult to participate in the learning process, that is, in the sharing of knowledge.

I have been observing the meetings in this conference since we began. I have been trying to see, for example, how many people from the African continent are here with us to follow what we are talking about and to take this knowledge, this information, to their people, so that they can be ready to work with those from other continents on the strategies we are talking about.

In fact you can see that the participation of Africans is very low. Why? Because, first of all, they do not have enough information to understand the value and the content of these meetings. But even if they did understand, they are poor, and they cannot travel here to attend.

By the way, I am not here to represent any of these people or countries. I live in the United States, but they need to know what we are talking about. And in order to share knowledge, we need also to think about the alleviation of the poverty, providing the income that can bring all of us together in order to discuss certain important issues, such as knowledge and the environment.

Another problem is the language barrier. In the last analysis, we see that English is the dominant language here. I am wondering how many people we took from the French-speaking part of Africa for these meetings. I think none. Why? Because of the language problem.

So you can see the challenge in your work of trying to duplicate your experiment in other parts of the world whose language is not English also.

Clovis Maksoud: I just want to make very preliminary, semantic comments, partly in view of my experience as the director of the Center for the Global South at the American University in Washington, D.C.

First, I hope Professor Dasgupta would try in the near future to use the term, South, rather than "Third World," because the latter does not obtain anymore in a concrete sense.

Second, the speakers have been talking this morning about the concept of knowledge, that of course is a weapon of power at times, but also a weapon of influence. There is always that sort of gray zone between people who influence events and people who dispose with power. And the academic community must be in a position to speak with influence—the influence of the intellect, of research, and of teaching.

Third, I believe that we have to make clearer the distinction between knowledge and information. Information is an ingredient of knowledge, but it is not knowledge, not even cumulatively.

What is the mechanism that transforms information into knowledge? In fact this is where research and teaching come into play, helping to analyze, sift, and sort out the information and determine what is relevant. The process is one of the most challenging elements in teaching or an academic institution. In the era of "CNN-ization" we are instantly informed about many events that are taking place. But are we equally knowledgeable? It is a crucial question that now occupies many academic centers and is an aspect of the research that we at the Center for the Global South are doing.

Another consideration is that in order to sift and determine what is relevant in information for knowledge, the objective must be focused. Why do we need knowledge? For what purpose? Finding the answers to these questions brings a growing awareness of the interdisciplinary nature of knowledge and education.

For instance I teach international law at American University, but I find myself branching out into being a little bit of an economist, an environmentalist, and a human rights specialist. By contrast, the structure of my early educational pursuits does not become very relevant in the new globalized economy and the globalization of issues.

I wanted to point out that as we see the various UN conferences that have been taking place, the Global South countries all have insisted that there is no such thing as simply environment issues, or issues of human rights, or women, or population. Every single UN conference has been population and development, and environment and development.

So in a similar way the specificities of our exact disciplines have to be in one form or another integrated into a coherent approach to our development. This is a particularly striking requirement in the Global South countries; hopefully the universities in the northern countries will try to bring about an integrated, interdisciplinary approach, not at the expense of particularities and specializations, but enhancing them to be plugged into an overall discipline.

Partha Dasgupta: Responding to my colleague from the Congo: yes, it is very sad and you are absolutely right. None of us speaks French. Some of us cannot speak English very well either, by the way. So we have to exclude French-speaking Africa. There is nothing I can do about it.

But since you raise the question, I must answer you with some degree of satisfaction: there is a way out. And this is the idea: If in the next two to three years it is possible to produce something like a largish textbook, written in a style based on the experience that we have, prompted by this experience, plus the illustrations—and it may be possible to have that happen—then the teaching might become more routinized.

In fact much of the art of teaching has been to make it possible for larger and larger volumes of people to imbibe the knowledge by actually routinizing the method of the teaching. Now that has its costs, and given the makeups of the people here, you will see the costs. But the benefits are also large. We have a lot of people who are educated today, and in the Golden Age, when everybody knew everything, they were not.

In response to some of the earlier remarks I should also suggest that I am not entirely convinced that the growing specialization so many of us have been commenting on is actually happening. We may start believing it, and there is always a momentum to a belief. But if you read in my subject, for instance, when I look at issues of the *Economic Journal* back in the 1920s and 1930s, they are unbelievably boring and extremely narrow. I mean, the authors of applied articles were just about as dull and as narrowly focused as possible.

By comparison if you wish to do a piece of applied work today, in let us say, labor economics or environmental economics, you have to be at least in touch with three or four disciplines. You need to know quite a bit of mathematics, statistics, and econometrics, for example. And you need to know labor law.

Furthermore, if you are going to publish in a top refereed journal, and you need to do that in order to advance your career, then you should know the subjects more than superficially, because otherwise some anonymous referee will say this person does not know what he or she is talking about.

In writing on demographic problems, as I have had to do in the last two or three years, I have had to learn something like three disciplines. I have had to learn a great deal on nutrition science, for example, because you just need to understand what is known currently about the effects on the nourishment on body size, and therefore, the possibilities of what is involved in terms of birthweight. I see no evidence of such interdisciplinary work 60 years ago in the *Economic Journal* or in the *American Economic Review*.

I get a similar reaction when I speak to my colleagues in molecular biology. They are telling me that they have to become much broader than their teachers were. You cannot do biochemistry without knowing crystallography, which requires a good deal of physics, and so forth.

So I am not entirely convinced that we have gone down the narrow, specialized path. I see things differently.

Audience comment: Yes and no. I think you have just heard a very good example of a very broad and widely read academic person, but I'm afraid to say he is not typical, and it is a great problem. As he says, if you are going to become good at something, you now have to learn several disciplines, and what that is telling us is that the problem areas that are emerging require people to have such a background.

But the human capital investment of doing this is enormous, and if a subject area fades, ceasing to become interesting, you have invested many, many years in acquiring knowledge that you now have to apply to something else.

I am not saying this is a good or a bad thing, but it is occurring. For example, I was 27 when I first had a job. That is, I had spent 10 years after school becoming an academic. Today, in some areas, you would be 37. That is, there would be an extra 10 years of knowledge to acquire. It is very expensive to do that. The training regimes really do not exist; you have to do it yourself.

We have instituted something called the post-doctoral fellowship, which did not exist before the Second World War. People now have several experiences at being a post-doctoral fellow before they emerge, in their late 30s, in the area in which they are going to specialize, such as molecular biology or environmental economics. They had to acquire more and more knowledge along the way. But it makes them more specialized. If the specialty ceases to be important, they will then have to look elsewhere.

As I say, it is yes and no. Greater knowledge is true, and yet, there are terrible problems with it.

Obligations of Academic Leaders to the Demands of Sustainable Development

Wadi Haddad

From many years of work in this field I am more and more convinced that there is a consistent life path for areas that get incorporated into the family of development. We start with economic development and then add human development, women in development, population development, and then environment in development.

Actually the development community is a very conservative one. It is like an aristocracy that does not like to marry into other families. All of these new development areas start with a passion, a love, an advocacy, even some irrationality to them. They do not get co-opted unless there is rigor and strong knowledge, and real justification.

What I have noticed is that to sustain the existence and the incorporation of a concern in the development area, knowledge is very important. We can say that knowledge sustains environmentally sustainable development.

I also notice from experience that if things stay at the advocacy and strong commitment level the situation creates conflicts among the members, because it becomes like a zero sum game. Knowledge can bring rationality into the connectivity, the integration, and the interdependence that characterize the development process.

I am sure we all agree that for environmentally sustainable development, knowledge is no luxury. It is indispensable.

These thoughts should set the stage for a very challenging topic, the obligations of academic leaders to the demands of sustainable development.

Panelist Remarks

Alvaro Umana

I would like to begin with the very simple proposition that academic leaders have difficulty with environmentally and socially sustainable development: first, because they do not understand it, with a few notable exceptions as we have heard here, and second, because the structures are wrong.

Regarding the latter point, the structures of the universities lock us into a disciplinary approach. Universities and academic institutions are inherently conservative and therefore hard to change. This fact poses some real problems to sustainability.

Another key problem is that sustainable development is much more knowledge-intensive than traditional development. The example that I will use for this is not complicated and is taking place all over the tropical world. It requires only a chain saw and an uneducated peasant, or a logger, to destroy a forest. On the other hand it takes an incredible amount of knowledge in many different areas to be able to subsist and derive income sustainably from that forest without destroying it.

Knowledge Needs of Sustainability

Although applied knowledge generated the chain saw, today we need much more sophisticated knowledge to carry us beyond the chain saw to the integration of a very large number of actions. Why? Because no single activity from the forest is economically sufficient for people to live sustainably from the forest. Whether it is logging, the extraction of sustainable products such as

nuts or vines, biodiversity prospecting, or selling water rights—none of these activities alone can ensure sustainable livelihoods.

If we can articulate this array of activities and the knowledge behind it in an adequate way, the composite does yield viable development, and leads to a completely changed person.

We have had some experience with this process in Costa Rica, for example, with the para-taxonomists. These people are peasants who have gone through a three-month training course to learn to be collectors of biological specimens.

The peasants not only derive a slightly higher income from this activity but also develop a specialized skill. Their children are not going to be para-taxonomists, though. Their children will be full biologists, because their parents will want their offspring to go through the professional training that they did not have. The knowledge that the peasants derive through this experience is what triggers their growth and their thoughts for their children's future.

If we recognize that sustainable development is much more knowledge-intensive, we have to focus on key questions: What types of knowledge are required? What are the demands in providing it? The problem is that the knowledge does not fit into traditional academic disciplines. In addition parts of the needed knowledge are only now being generated.

We have the two themes, therefore, as emphasized by this meeting: How do we integrate cutting-edge knowledge, and how do we mainstream sustainability in educational programs?

Science is always required in the basic components of sustainable development. We need physics, chemistry, and biology to be able to put together what people might call ecosystem science or conservation science or, in a more grandiose formulation, Earth system science.

However, this is just the beginning. We also need economics, and Partha Dasgupta has done a very good job of explaining the challenges in valuation, identifying tradeoffs, and analyzing costs and benefits and the price tag of effective regulation.

Shortcomings of Traditional Economics

From my perspective several things that traditional economics lacks need to be taught in environmental or ecological economics.

First, economists do not think about the scale of the system, except in terms of economies of scale. They do not think about the scale of the activity with respect to the size of the ecosystem.

Traditional economics is also too short term-oriented as a consequence of choices for the discount rate, so we have to introduce the essence of sustainability, which looks to the long run. We have to introduce ways to handle long-run problems, or projects that have long-term payoffs, as sustainable projects do.

Furthermore, the role of energy and materials is not properly taught in economics, although all the principles are known. This is actually done very well in courses such as Partha described.

Traditional economics also does not properly address the valuation of environmental services. Too many economists still think that air and water are free goods. New rules of economics must be introduced to insure that the value of an ecosystem is not taken as zero unless these values are demonstrated to be very, very small. In fact we have to start saying in economics that ecosystem values are positive and non-negligible unless proven otherwise.

Another critical shortcoming deals with the relationship of the different components of capital. Traditionally, they are considered substitutes. However, the argument of very easy substitutability has not held up. Now we tend to look at capital in four ways: natural capital, regular manmade capital, social capital, and human capital. We also have to look at the interactions among those different components. As we know, the World Bank has come around on this.

Then there are the input and output rules that say that we cannot take out of a living ecosystem more than its natural regeneration rate will allow, and that we cannot dump more pollutants in than its natural regeneration rate will allow cleanup.

All of these considerations need to be integrated into economics teaching for knowledge and understanding about sustainable development.

In addition, though, we really need to teach management—the practicalities of how organizations operate. We need to teach a new concept of bottom-up participatory approaches, but no one is now teaching it. Indeed there is a whole technology of participation that needs work.

The Bank itself has tremendous problems with this. Its environment and resettlement operational directives are very participatory on paper, but participation is not about just calling one meeting and then forgetting about it.

Finally, we also need to teach public policy, because in sustainable development there are problems that cannot be taken up by anybody except the state itself. Examples include population control, the management of territory, land use planning, energy systems, and water supply. These are all beyond a micro approach.

How can academic institutions respond? How could they integrate the demands—the needs—about which I am speaking now?

A Special Academic Program

My answer is based on my own experience of the past five years, which is the creation of a two-year master's program on sustainable development within the context of a school of business and management. This, by the way, has some advantages for academic or traditional universities and also some disadvantages.

I have also participated in a series of workshops promoted by the Gilman Foundation where we considered the experience of Yale, Michigan, Cornell, and Duke, all of which are trying to provide interdisciplinary groups on environment and development.

At our school some things we talked about in the beginning included the importance of opening up research opportunities for faculty, and identifying and creating interdisciplinary groups or seminars that could lead to the development of curricula.

In fact the key issue is how to develop appropriate curricula that integrate cutting-edge knowledge that then spreads beyond the courses themselves and eventually reaches the entire university population. Of course this is easier in a school of business and management than in a whole university that has many, many programs.

Our own experience was launched at Rio five years ago, and it is still the only such program within the context of a business school. It has attracted, so far, more than 100 students from 18 countries and it has graduated about 80 students. We have a common first year for all students and a second differentiated year offering courses in the economics of resources and pollution, sustainable economic development, management of protected areas, energy and materials management, benefit-cost analysis, and environmental input assessment, as well as a course on policy, planning, and legislation for sustainability.

The experience has been interesting. It was an uphill battle at the beginning but we have seen the enrollments increase through the years. This year close to 25 percent of the total student population has chosen our option. The effort has been made possible by outside funding, including several foundations.

Lessons and Results

What have we learned? For one thing we have found a wide variety of interests in our program, from many disciplines. We attract students who come primarily with a science, agronomy, or forestry background, but we also draw lawyers and sociologists. The challenge is how to create a uniform base of knowledge because, for example, the science students may have the background needed for one component of the studies but not for the other.

The difficulties in gaining acceptance for the new program have not been from lack of demand, but, rather, from the old faculty and students who feel threatened by innovation. This is why successfully launching a program such as this, within an institution, seems to require an untouchable senior faculty to champion it. If we try to hire a new person to head the program, other faculty members will destroy him or her, because the new person will be doing things not rewarded, traditionally, by any of the disciplines.

Therefore it takes somebody who already has a reputation, or who has a very strong position in the university, to take this on in the beginning—then the resistance decreases slowly, over time, and the interest among the rest of the students starts to increase. As an example, our course on energy and materials management, while only mandatory for a small group, was taken recently by more half of the entire student population, simply because they thought this was a good course for them.

Finally, the most important result of an effort such as ours occurs when sustainability is mainstreamed into the rest of the courses and into the teaching of business students in general. We are at this stage right now.

Panelist Remarks

Veena Das

I am going to be speaking in some ways very much from my perspective in the Delhi School of Economics and Delhi University where I have taught for the last 30 years.

It seems to me that the question of sustainable development has to deal with the fact that we have now, increasingly, global institutions with globally set, agreed-upon norms, and we have local knowledge applications that frequently must take place primarily in the context of implementation of these norms.

On the one hand people like me who work in universities in the South must deal with writers who would argue that the conceptual tasks of thinking in fact have all been worked out in Europe, and that the virtues that are necessary for universities now are those of courage, or of applying knowledge that is in fact already known.

In an example from my point of view as an anthropologist, I concluded some years ago that normally we write in a way that makes a local world available for consumption, if you will, by a kind of international or national community of scholars, and I gave my students the task of supposing that we were doing the reverse.

Suppose, I suggested to the students, that we were saying that the world of bureaucracy, of courts of law, of international institutions, had to be the research object, and that we had to make this knowledge available to people in slums and resettlement colonies, in New Delhi.

I found that in fact it was extremely difficult to produce this kind of research because these institutions, that are in some ways consumers of knowledge, are very rarely available for people like us to study and to make this kind of knowledge available to those who, in their own way, have access to these institutions.

Experience of Bhopal

This was brought home very sharply to me during the Bhopal disaster, in which almost nothing was known by our people about the methyl isocyanate that leaked in dangerous quantities. In the courts of law, however, everyone had to speak from a position of supposed certainty; the people who had suffered from the leak, who had absolutely no doubts that they were suffering and who thought the proof was there in the chemical's damage to their bodies, found it quite incredible that in the courts they were in fact completely silenced.

Therefore, it does seem to me that there are very difficult questions regarding the apparent consensus about sustainable development. Where is the place for local institutions and local knowledge in this issue? Must we assume that these local institutions, such as universities in the South, only have the role of being recipients and consumers of knowledge that others produce, or is their own production of knowledge to have any sense and meaning in defining locally sustainable development?

Obviously, when I am talking about global and local, this is not a matter of scale as I understand scale. This is much more a question of perspective and, in a way, a perspective from which you could assume that sometimes, viewing through a small frame allows the eye to roam at a very large scale.

I would not necessarily say that one position is narrower while another is wider, or that one reality is at the higher level and one is at the lower level. On the contrary there are very different perspectives available from the same point where one may be standing. I am always impressed by Foucault's notion that truth is not just waiting in the darkness on which we will shed some light—instead it may be found through a different way of speaking.

To continue, our experience at the Delhi school with some ways of thinking about sustainable development in such issues as health and environment has been that certain kind of perspectives deriving from local contexts in fact tend to be completely silenced.

I have already given the example of Bhopal that by wide agreement was the largest industrial disaster known in this century. By the way, it was amazing how quickly closure came to the kind of research and knowledge that were to be generated in that case, especially for the victims.

Another example keeps coming up again and again. It regards the apparent success of global institutions in creating healthy environments. In fact, the eradication of smallpox was one case where the global institutions were able to marshal local knowledge. It is very interesting to me that in the whole process the date by which the disease had to eradicated was set by global institutions. There was very little national consultation on this critical matter.

Need for a Local Voice

Second, consider that in several countries vaccinators went in the villages and sometimes broke into houses, tied up people, and gave them vaccines. Now it is true that the eradication was very successful, and it points to the fact that technocratic solutions can work, and work very well. Nevertheless, it is amazing to me that we did not ask what happens to serenity, to citizenship, to informed consent, everything which is said to be central in thinking about bioethics and about enlightened medical research.

My sense is that globally defined goals will silence a lot of questions unless people in the countries in which these goals are to be carried out are able to express these concerns in some ways for the international community to think about.

I am not saying that this unfortunate result is inevitable, that serenity or citizenship or informed consent will necessarily be violated. In fact we saw the polio eradication program shift in two important ways. First, it was felt that people needed a stake in the program. Second, the dates by which the world could be declared free from polio were changed and that additional time was used to educate mothers, helping them to eliminate the illness and save children.

I am saying, however, that top-heavy global policies have seemed to be inevitable. If local questions are not posed, then purely applying a certain kind of knowledge and consensus is likely to be disastrous in the long run for countries who now have to be made safe because of the threat of the travel of disease.

The second example that I want to give is this: The way we think about these issues and try to prioritize the claims of those who may benefit from a new knowledge and technology has had very important results.

For instance, if we think about immunization, it is not purely the vaccine in the bottle that constitutes the technology. The scope of the technology also includes administrative apparatuses, and the ways by which people will or will not receive the vaccine in local political cultures.

Taking a New Perspective on Technology

The feedback—that is, looking at the technology from the point of view of consumption rather than just production—has led to some very helpful techniques, such as needles that will bend after one use so that nurses cannot use them again and again, or ways to show whether the vaccine is efficacious. These may seem to be very small-scale innovations but they were in fact of absolute importance in trying to assure that vaccines were effective. Thus it is through constant feedback that some very interesting and important conceptual developments happen.

My third point is that as we develop globally defined norms, it may very well be that what is of local urgency will be totally ignored. For instance, in the case of smallpox eradication, we know that for two years the primary health staffs from the affected countries were taken off all other health delivery programs. They were taken off family planning and nutritional work, as well as a whole series of other programs so that the vaccination program could succeed. The cost of that policy action has yet to be calculated. Thus, some matters that are of local urgency tend not to be considered at all in the global consensus.

I will give you another very telling example. Heroic efforts are made to introduce a mass immunization program for Hepatitis B. Of course, it is important to introduce the effort in this way so that the cost of vaccines can be kept lower. Hepatitis C, which is an intractable disease and tends to be problematic for local populations, is in fact low on the agenda of global research.

Challenges in Defining Competence

My final point is this: Partha Dasgupta spoke eloquently about creating a very important professional group of economists, but there are assumptions in this idea that we need to look at very seriously.

One of the assumptions would seem to be a certain hierarchy in the sense that publications in journals in the West would indicate greater competence and would convey greater prestige or status on that person than on someone publishing in local languages or publishing in local or national level journals.

I see no easy way out of this, because indeed in some places professional journals have probably had a very bad reputation, and therefore there are very difficult questions about quality and standards. No doubt the very processes of knowledge include ways of ranking universities and scholars.

It does seem to me, though, that there are great difficulties flowing from the manner in which competence is defined. One of the consequences can be that methods or procedures of training that are translatable into either national or local uses will be increasingly difficult to implement. For instance, we have a problem in the Delhi School of Economics. A number of our alumni are now teaching in the United States and we are unable to persuade them to come back and do research with us.

These are the points I would like to put on the table. One, I argue that it may be too early to conclude that all serious conceptual thinking has been done. Two, I contend that it is also too early to assume that all the conceptual questions will be asked in universities outside the South. We need, quite seriously, and not only as a rhetorical strategy, to think about ways by which questions that might be of very great national or local importance can be taken up.

The Critical Path: Linking Knowledge to Advance Environmentally and Socially Sustainable Development

Kenneth Prewitt

Think back 40 years, when the topic on the table was development, before its now fashionable adjective—sustainable—was routinely attached. Recall the "Five-Year Plans" favored in the early phases of what we then called the new nations, with pride of place in those plans being given to capital accumulation and investment. Recall as well the importance assigned to the natural resource base. The nations that would advance steadily and rapidly were those richly endowed in minerals, forests, good soils, and water. In this thinking, more was expected of Indonesia than of Japan, of Republic of Congo than of Morocco, of Brazil than of Mexico.

Education in the Context of Development

Education was not absent, of course, but it was assigned a supportive, even peripheral role. Not so today. In the course of 40 years education has moved from the periphery to the center of thinking about development.

Educational themes march under various terms—including, especially, human capital and, more recently, the metaphor of capacity building. It is now commonplace to assert that development flows from a growth in the competence of a society to apply modern science and technology. This growth in competency must be lodged both in individuals and institutions. These linked competencies—individual and institutional—are nurtured first and foremost in a nation's educational practices.

I certainly do not mean to suggest that only in the last decade or so has knowledge and competency been seen as central to economic growth. One of the lessons we learn from history is that the great push by Western exploration into the Americas and Africa, when it was primarily motivated by wealth-seeking, actually generated less wealth than when it was motivated by knowledge-seeking. The fur traders explored the upper Missouri River in the American west, but real development followed the meticulous scientific expedition of Lewis and Clark. A similar pattern unfolded in West Africa, where the earlier wealth-seeking entrepreneurs trading in gold and slaves left much destruction but little development. Not until the Niger exploration concentrated on the natural, navigational, and geographic sciences was there development in the sense that we talk about it today.

The generalization of the hypothesis that knowledge-seeking is wealth-producing comes today from sociologists who write of the "knowledge society" and economists who offer "new growth theory." We coin the term knowledge workers. To history and theory are added the lessons of recent economic achievements. Here the stress on the centrality of professional competencies, human performance, and an educated labor force for economic growth argues from the experience of Japan, and then of the East Asian tigers.

All of this theorizing and practice has worked the notion of human resources deep into thinking about development, becoming the orthodoxy of the 1990s. This orthodoxy has been deepened and expanded in parallel with the now nearly universal replacement of the term development with that of sustainable development. Many wise things have already been said in this conference about the advance in conceptual richness and complexity that has occurred as we have all come to take for granted that what matters is not development but sustainable development.

It has led to economic theorizing about the right way to "charge the economy for the consumption of its resource endowment" (Solow). It has led to ethical theorizing about what is fair and right in the cross-generational allocation of costs and benefits. It has led to improved political theorizing about how to secure public goods when the goods are transboundary and even global in scope. It has led to new social theories about reciprocal obligations and social cooperation.

Spin-offs from the Sustainable Development Concept

It has also, and most relevant for present purposes, led to hard thinking about what kind of individual and institutional competencies will be required of a world that wants to increase production and consumption, though not waste natural resources and not pollute and despoil ground, water, or air. That is, the concern that development must be sustainable has led to a fresh consideration of what kind of education and training is necessary.

It is not my assignment to explain sustainability, and I will slide easily past the ambiguities and difficulties of the term. Nevertheless, I should make a few if conventional points about sustainability before turning to the central task, which is to reflect on higher education in the context of sustainable development.

From the perspective taken in these comments, the important point about linking the term sustainable with development is how it has sensitized us to thinking about international public goods. It is this phrase—international public good—that I will focus on, but for now introduce it without much explication. The

most useful way to begin thinking about it is to turn first to more familiar ground—that is, to public goods and higher education at the national level.

Education as a Public Good

We have robust theories—as well as instrumentalities—available for thinking about public goods at the level of the nation-state. Here we readily recognize that there are collective benefits or public goods that, though in the social interest, are not in the interest of any one individual to pay for—given that they are goods that are, by their nature, nonexclusive and thus open to free rider.

How then can we ensure that a nation provides public goods? We empower the nation-state to compensate for market failures, to discourage negative externalities, and to solve the problem of the free rider. This empowerment takes the form of obligatory taxation and state regulation.

That is, the combined powers of taxation and regulation are integral to the ability of the nation-state to provide public goods. The nation-state can create an overland transport system by combining state financing and the right of eminent domain. It can create an infrastructure for research and development through public finance of research universities and national laboratories, and can ensure that ideas are not captured through practices and procedures that guarantee open intellectual exchange. All of this is common knowledge.

For present purposes we underline the assumption that higher education—at least elements of it under some circumstances—are treated as public goods and thus benefit from public investment. That is, to the extent that the educational system produces a social as well as individual return to investment there is a social interest in subsidizing that system.

This is not the place to get into the intricacies of return-on-investment analysis. Suffice it to say that a number of key institutions continue to assume that there is sufficient social return to justify public investment—generally an investment that will emphasize research over teaching, the laboratory sciences over the less capital-intensive fields, and advanced over baccalaureate education.

The investment in research derives from the assumption that the benefits are not appropriated by pre-designated individuals. Research is funded because it is assumed that new knowledge—whether in science and technology, art and literature, or philosophy and music—accrues to the society at large. This is especially true when the social benefits are difficult to anticipate or measure or are stretched out over a long timeframe. Thus, public money is invested in epidemiology and public health, or in basic science, or in specialties that are thought potentially important but for which no market value can yet be assigned, such as oceanography or outer space.

Investment in the laboratory sciences or those that require extensive field observation—such as area studies or ecology—because they are capital-intensive thus unsubsidized—would generate a fee structure so high as to be a disincentive to bright students selecting among alternative fields of study.

Investment is made in graduate more than in undergraduate education, because for graduate education, especially, although not only, in the laboratory sciences, the unit costs are high and the benefits are not easily captured by investors or individual students. In contrast undergraduate education leads to large private benefits, easily captured, at a lower initial cost.

By the way, though public goods theory justifies public investment in higher education, it does not follow that there should be public universities. To take the United States as the obvious example: government-sponsored research and graduate education is every bit as present in the great private universities—Harvard, Hopkins, Chicago, Stanford—as in the public universities—Michigan, California. What is less clear is what happens to a public good investment when higher education not only privatizes, but also becomes profit-seeking. Early indications are that profit-making institutions favor courses of study and types of training that generate relatively higher private value and relatively lower social value.

A case in point is the Philippines, where many prospective students (or their families) have calculated that the return to higher education makes it a worthwhile investment of private funds. This has led to a demand that has been responded to by the private sector, including a number of for-profit educational institutions. Indeed, these institutions now outnumber both public and private nonproprietary higher education institutions. Science education, and graduate training more generally, does not feature prominently in the programs of for-profit institutions, and often not even in other private sector universities and colleges supported by philanthropic funds or student fees.

This situation, not restricted to the Philippines, is troubling for the subject at hand. For whatever else sustainable development might mean, it certainly presupposes an understanding and application of modern science and technology—including an understanding of how not to apply modern technologies. But scientific and technological fields are high cost, and the return on private investment—with its promise of near-term and largely individual-level benefits—will not lead to necessary funds. Public goods require public subsidies.

Thinking about Public Goods at the International Level

I will return to this issue subsequently, but we should now move from commentary focused at the national level to commentary at the international level, for it is here that the issues of sustainable development begin to bite. A significant number of specific issues that travel under the umbrella of sustainable development are what can be called international public goods, that is, they provide collective benefits that have the properties they do because they are transboundary.

Bear in mind that in public-goods theory the individual actor who cannot capture the benefits of a given investment or cost can be a nation-state as well as a person or firm. Obviously, then, as we shift from the nation-state level to the international level we encounter the complicating fact that the nation is going to be a reluctant investor in creating a good that has the free rider problem. What incentive, then, exists to produce international public goods?

Compounding the difficulty are the negative externalities, when behaviors in one country pose dangers and costs to another. How, then, to create a system of surveillance to detect such externalities, and to impose some sort of control over them?

As noted earlier, there are generally two classes of issues addressed in public-goods thinking. One class of such issues is suggested by what some scholars see as market failures associated with the globalization in manufacturing, production, and finance. The argument goes as follows: Global enterprises have an incentive to seek venues in which they can minimize payment of taxes or escape burdens of regulation (that is, escape those legal and financial arrangements designed to contribute to public goods for nation-states). This is what makes global enterprises competitive in the international marketplace. Why should a profit-making clothier not make cheaper jeans with child labor? Why should a profit-making chemical enterprise not manufacture where toxic wastes can be drained into the local river? Especially why should they not if their competitors are taking advantage of cheap labor and unregulated manufacturing processes? Moral suasion may limit particularly excessive instances, but if competitive capitalism is the dynamic engine of growth it is purported to be, it is doubtful that the world should rely on self-restraint by commercial enterprises.

Obviously, and non-trivially, it can be in the interest of individual firms to accede to binding regulations that govern all firms. The Pure Food and Drug Act in the United States, for instance, reflected the interests of some firms in international trade. The exporters benefited from a United States guarantee that products were free of toxic properties. They cooperated with a regulation that solved the free rider problem—no United States producer would cheat in the domestic market, and in the meantime they could export because overseas consumers had confidence in United States manufacturing processes.

The regulatory state and the welfare state with which we are familiar in North America and Western Europe represents a century of sustained attention to labor exploitation, consumer fraud, unsafe products, environmental damage, occupational dangers, monopolistic control, collusion, and discarded workers. To redress these excesses the state has provided any number of protections and programs—consumer protection, laws against child labor, unemployment insurance, anti-trust regulation, and clean air and water laws. These protections and programs impose costs on commercial enterprises, costs which become unaffordable if their international competitors are not under similar obligations. The attempt to internationalize such obligations is slow-going (the NAFTA fight is a good recent example).

There is a second category of issues routinely incorporated under the heading of international public goods: the familiar class of goods that are necessarily global or transnational, that is, that cannot be provided by nation-states or even regions acting on their own. Most familiar here, of course, is the environmental agenda: global warming, acid rain, invasive species, and biodiversity loss. Also included are the health and population agenda—infectious emergent diseases and population growth insofar as it leads to noncontrollable migratory flows. Even security thinkers sometimes invoke the theory of international public goods: thus proliferation of weapons of mass destruction wherein country A making weapons available to country B puts at risk countries C through N, and the at-risk countries can control countries A and B only by framing the issue at the global level.

How to Secure Public Goods without Regulatory and Taxation Powers

Two points are very clear about international public goods, and they both derive from the absence of an authority that can operate transnationally.

First, it is difficult to establish international regulatory regimes, though of course this is what is at stake in the Biodiversity Convention, even though it is framed as soft law and is careful to enshrine the principle of national sovereignty in its stance against interference with national development. The establishment of international regulatory regimes is at stake with the Global Warming Convention, which reaches toward targets and timetables. It is present in the environmental riders to free-trade regimes. It is present in the norm setting of the World Health Organization. Indeed, standards and norms have become a soft version of international regulatory regimes. To suggest that it is difficult is to not to suggest that these regimes are absent, only to take due notice that what we take for granted at the nation-state level as regards state regulatory powers is simply not available currently to the world community, and probably will not be available any time soon. I note this empirically and not to pass judgment.

If regulatory regimes are difficult to establish, this is even more true for international public finance instrumentalities. There being no global government (or one in sight) there is, by definition, no international taxing authority. Short of an international taxing authority, are there more efficient and more just ways to acquire international funds than the current system of bilateral aid and quasi-voluntary contributions to international agencies? The debt-swap instrument is a small but telling example of innovations in this regard; the trading permits now much discussed as we approach Kyoto are as well. There are the various tax proposals, such as the Tobin tax on international financial transactions or sin taxes that would be internationally collected. That these are but gestures does not make them trivial, but they are gestures. It is easier for world leaders to convene in Beijing, Cairo, Rio, and Stockholm and pronounce this, that, or the other global need—sustainable development, women's reproductive health, water, and habitat—than it is to figure out how to pay for these praiseworthy goals.

Education as an International Public Good

These observations about international public goods—their importance is matched only by the difficulty of realizing them—brings us to the obvious question about higher education.

We start with a simple point that follows directly on the previous comment. Education can easily be conceptualized as a global public good in exactly the sense that it generates collective benefits that are nonexclusionary and therefore cannot be captured only by those who invest in education. Nevertheless, there is no international standard setting or public finance system that even remotely approaches higher education as a global public good. This is not likely to change in our professional lifetimes.

Yet it is easy to make the case for international public goods in the educational sector. I will put three components on the table:

1. A research and development system that addresses problems of global significance where knowledge would benefit all or most nations
2. An information and expert system that can sustain a process of shared learning across countries
3. Harmonized norms and standards for evaluating such "products" as ideas or professional certification that increasingly are used in transnational transactions.

Our interest here is not in chasing the fantasy of creating a high standard, internationally funded higher education system that produces people and ideas suitable for realizing globally significant collective benefits. Rather, our interest is the more modest interest of asking what features of higher education—viewed as an international public good—might advance globally significant R&D, information systems, and standard setting. In particular what might be of interest to the international donor community and to the administrators of higher education in the nation-states of the world?

Education Agenda

With respect to education several things merit attention. First, there is an important international flow of students. This is an uneven flow with certain countries—the United States and the countries of Western Europe—as points of destination for students from around the world. I do not make light of the lumpiness of the flows, but in the majority of countries of the world it is possible to take courses from a faculty that is not native to the country, and to have classmates that are not native to that country. These possibilities do not reach the probabilities they do in the United States, where in certain technical fields the chances are fifty-fifty that the instructor in the classroom is not an American and the chances are fifty-fifty that the person in the seat next to you is not an American. Though the probabilities are lower, the incidence of this pattern is not negligible in countries across the globe: Kenya and South Africa; Holland and Germany; India and Australia; Mexico and Argentina. Every major higher education system in the world invites and actively recruits international students. In proportion and in absolute numbers this flow has not been well mapped, but anecdotal evidence suggests it is steadily increasing.

Second, the Internet and distance learning are making likely the distribution of common teaching materials around the globe. That is, topics such as the science of global warming and the economics of addressing it are now packaged and distributed in a way that can create a global curriculum. The megauniversities are a vehicle for this distribution. These are huge: nearly 600,000 students are enrolled in Anadolu University in Turkey, and more than 500,000 are enrolled in the China TV university. The ten largest megauniversities around the world have a combined enrollment of 2.5 million students.

It would be easy to overstate such trends, but it would not do to ignore them either. Education has always been about the "national project," about educating a common citizenry in the values, traditions, and practices of the place in which the education occurs. Globe-trotting at part of the educational experience, combined with curricular materials designed for a global market, adds something important to the national project. That which is added is less parochial, less about the local experience, and more about global challenges and opportunities.

Insofar as dealing with sustainable development requires educated citizens that share some common knowledge and presumptions, this deparochialization is a contributing factor. Higher education funders and administrators can adopt policies that impede or facilitate, retard or accelerate. Issues as simple as recognizing credits earned elsewhere, or providing opportunities for foreign language achievement, can tilt toward the facilitating and accelerating.

Research Agenda

There are also a number of trends on the research front that, if supported, can accelerate the capacity of our knowledge-base to make its needed contribution to sustainable development.

There is first a strong if uneven research capacity around the world; it is the unevenness, of course, that we need to worry about. We all know the numbers, with a progressive drop-off in per capita scientists and scholars as we move from Euro-America to Asia and Latin America and then to the Middle East and Africa. The Russian Federation has a reasonably high per capita, but is crippled by the collapse of scientific infrastructure over the last half-dozen years. There are scattered efforts to redress the imbalances, but these efforts are neither systematic nor well-funded. Here a program for African economists, there a program for Russian mathematicians, elsewhere a program for soil scientists or medical research. I do not make light of these efforts, but as best we can tell, they really are scattered, responsive to particular programmatic interests of private foundations or bilateral aid agencies or the multilateral banks.

Reflecting as well as trying to compensate for this unevenness of intellectual capacity around the world is the growth of important research networks. The International Panel on Climate Change (IPCC) is prominent in this regard; as is the somewhat looser network of the Consultative Group on International Agricultural Research (CGIAR) system, and even less well-developed networks in disease research or epidemiology. There are also global research projects in fields such as oceanography, plate tectonics, and space exploration. These networks and projects do produce knowledge that is available to scientific communities everywhere, whether or not they participate in producing it. This is buttressed by an impressive if still premature growth in virtual libraries of scientific and scholarly journals, and in the wide sharing of research results over the Internet. Of course, there are serious problems of access.

Networks and related globally significant scholarly resources are comparatively more advanced in the natural sciences than in the social sciences, and the social sciences in turn are more advanced than the humanities. From the perspective of sustainable development, this disciplinary unevenness is to be lamented. That the issues of sustainable development are matters of social organization, political incentives, and human motivation is self-evident. That they raise the most profound ethical questions is equally evident. But international investment has largely concentrated on the physical properties of sustainable development—matters of atmosphere, soils, and water. Some greater balance in the intellectual apparatus we bring to bear is in order.

Final note should be taken of the advantages and disadvantages of English as the emerging universal language of the scientific and scholarly community. The great advantage, of course, is that there is a common language. A disadvantage is that it advantages scientists for whom English is the first language, but a more severe disadvantage is that it gradually denies to scholarship those truths that can only be grasped by studying local cultures, histories, and practices in the languages in which they find their human meaning.

Encouraging Beginnings

In conclusion, in an embryonic form to be sure, we begin to see the makings of higher education practices that, if nurtured, can help in the generation of new knowledge and the deployment of existing knowledge to a new generation. This new knowledge will help us think through the sustainable development agenda at the global level. It will require public investment because it is a public good. We will have to organize a strategy for that public investment, as indeed the World Bank, UNESCO, and other international agencies presently have under review.

The Social–Natural Science Gap in Educating for Sustainable Development

Ismail Serageldin

I want to share with you my profound concern about the aspect of sustainable development that deals with the issue of the sciences, and what I perceive as the science gap that is growing around the world.

Fundamentally, I see not just a gulf, but a yawning gulf, between the industrialized countries and the developing countries in terms of sheer numbers of scientists and engineers. UNESCO tells us that per million we have about 2,800 scientists and engineers in the North, and, on average, about 200 or less in South Asia and Africa.

Another statistic is one that my friend, Henry Kendall of the Union of Concerned Scientists, quoted today at another conference session. Talking about biotechnology impacts, he said that there are 85 times more scientists in the United States than in Indonesia—and this is just the number. We are not talking about the extent and the quality of the training, the quality of the facilities at their disposal, or the amount of resources that the scientists have to work with.

This gap in numbers is staggering and it is growing. What is of particular concern is that we are in a global transformation that is not just connecting markets and economies, but that is moving us inexorably toward a knowledge-based society. While it will bring many wonderful things to many people, we know that the future also has a dark side.

Increase in Inequities

The knowledge-based society will lead to greater inequities, and ultimately a fraying of the social contract, unless purposeful actions are taken to protect equity while maintaining incentives.

We find, for example, that not only is the gap growing between the remuneration of computer programmers and lawyers versus carpenters and welders, but that the gap between the best and the worst computer programmers is infinitely greater than the gap between the best and the worst carpenters or welders.

This is part of a movement toward a stratified, inequitable society. That is why you can have a union of welders, but I doubt that you will ever have a union of computer programmers. It is not likely to work. We need new instruments, new visions.

This is happening within societies and between societies. The gap in the ability of societies to master knowledge is affected not only by resources and numbers of scientists but also by a number of other factors, including the transformation of proprietary science.

In these circumstances we need to learn from history. In this conference earlier this week I quoted from Karl Marx on globalization and the transformation of industry. I said that it is stunning to see how little things have changed. He predicted the increasing inequities that would occur, the pauperization of the proletariat, and how this was inherent in the structure existing at that time.

What Marx could not predict was that there would be sufficient resilience and imagination in the design of the institutions in the twentieth century to create the middle class. This did not result in the hyper-rich becoming poor, but it did result in a much greater spread in benefits than had been the case.

It is inconceivable that some today would argue that rising inequities—conditions of misery beneath my definition of human decency—are a necessary part of development. We are brought back to the nineteenth century to remember Charles Dickens and the painful stories of the kind he wrote. We are moved to ask: Why cannot we learn from the past and invent the institutional structures that will enable us to spread the benefits more widely in the twenty-first century?

This is a serious problem. The trends are global. Increasing connectivity and global interaction can have enormous advantages in terms of helping small countries and helping people in remote areas participate in the opportunities of the global marketplace and share in global knowledge. But there are also disadvantages. Beyond the issues of inequity in a knowledge-based society is the increasing possibility that knowledge-based elites in developing countries will be more connected with the world and become less and less engaged with their own societies. They will be intellectual expatriates who will have moved, not physically, but mentally, and in terms of affinity.

My perception is that there are a number of transformations taking place in the world today about which we know relatively little. This challenges me to go back to the issue of higher education.

For instance we are seeing the transformation of the knowledge paradigm itself. When I was a student, we had fairly distinct disciplines in science, such as physics, chemistry, and biology. This morning I was sitting with people who were talking about both physical chemistry and molecular biology, just one indication that the boundaries between the knowledge disciplines have disappeared. In place of the dividing line there is increasingly a seamless web of knowledge. Some of the more exciting change is actually taking place in the interstices of the former disciplines.

The knowledge paradigm, while not yet challenging the reductionist perspective of contemporary science, is experiencing much more fluid boundaries than a generation ago both in the accumulating of knowledge, such as research, and in the imparting of skills and knowledge, such as teaching in the university.

Possibility of a Positive New Era

This changing situation calls into question the paradigms by which the centers of learning in the developing countries define themselves and their mission, both as regards their own societies, and as regards the transforming global landscape.

It brings forth an awesome idea: We may indeed be on the cusp of a whole new era, and yes, I will use that hackneyed word, the millennium. In some ways it could become the millennium in the broad sense of the word, in that we might find ourselves with the tools to banish hunger, abolish some of the worst and most crippling diseases, create livable cities and sustainable agriculture, and promote the well-being of people.

What I see does not seem to indicate that we are moving in that direction, though. I am focusing on the developing countries in expressing this concern. Why? Because 80 percent of the world's population qualifies as "developing."

The question is: How are they going to organize themselves to cope with the transformation that is being willy-nilly created by various economic and institutional forces that are knowledge-driven? It is an absolutely critical issue, and the educational system—and within it, the university and its function—is fundamental and central in the picture.

History does not give us much encouragement, by the way. There is a widespread perception that universities, even in the industrialized North, have failed to adapt to much of this transformation that is sweeping the Earth.

Is this surprising? Consider the task: the adaptation of the knowledge paradigm in universities challenges us to rethink the structure and governance of the university, its relationship between the public and the private, its function as a custodian of certain societal values, and its function as a creator of skills for the labor force.

These are matters that come with particular acuity for the developing countries. For there the universities have a myth all their own. I challenged Veena Das yesterday on the question: What is the role of the university? Is it the beacon of light? Is it the center of social transformation? Is it an agent of change? Is it where the students come into contact with new and liberating ideas, where they search for their sense of identity, where they define the future in the crucible of their minds? Is the university simply a mill that is producing large numbers of mediocre people for government employment, or rejection by the private sector, as the case may be? Is it something that is an agent of change in society, or is it a perpetuator of certain existing structures? Clearly, the university is both catalyst for change and force for the status quo, but it is part of our challenge to ask why it should be more one than the other, and how it will play that role.

Change in Educational Traditions

It seems to me that if you look at the traditional functions of the university, there are basically three to be defined.

The first of these is a certification function. That is, students go through a university and then receive a degree that says that they have a bachelor's of engineering, bachelor's of science, whatever the degree is, certifying that they have acquired a certain amount of knowledge that should enable them to function in the labor market in a certain way.

We know, of course, that in the science-based disciplines, regardless of what is learned, the idea that a person could be certified for the next 30 or 40 years with the same skills has become totally laughable, not just obsolete. In fact almost all of the professional disciplines have set in motion alternative means of testing and certification, above and beyond the certification that the universities used to provide.

The university's certification function has been clearly challenged by the increasing perception in many parts of the world that there is no guaranteed job at the end of the university degree, and, hence, the valuation placed on that degree is called into question.

The second main function of the university has been what one could term, without excessive hyperbole, the search for truth, promoting a better understanding of the self and of knowledge, the expansion of knowledge, and doing so not from a politically hackneyed perspective that is subservient to whatever "truth" is popular at the moment.

This university role also is being called into question, because in the new, post-modern perspective, there are multiple frames of reference, and the very concept of an objective truth is being challenged, even in the scientific doctrines. Some of the post-modern critics are arguing that there may be no such thing as science beyond simply a specialized discourse.

A third aspect of the university, also called into question, has been the function of socialization and identity. It is at the university that we are formed, ultimately, to have a perception of ourselves as belonging to a particular society. It is there that our political opinions usually mature. It is there that we may engage in our first militant activities dealing with public issues, and it is there that friendships and other forms of affinities are born.

This historic function faces challenges, particularly in the developing world. On the one hand there is this tidal wave of globalization; on the other is a counterpoint of assertive specificity at the local level, that, in the extreme case, is an affirmation of the self at the expense of the other, sometimes going to the extremes of ethnic cleansing. Together, the globalization and the assertion of specificity have set adrift many university constructs that have traditionally helped to shape a common identity based on inclusiveness, tolerance, and openness.

A Stunning Crisis of Identity

In many developing countries universities are unable not just to rise to the challenges that I have described, but more critically, even to fulfill their old functions.

This identity crisis of the universities along with the degradation of many of the public institutions in the developing countries has, frankly, stunned me.

When I was considering college in Egypt, the idea of not going to Cairo University, the national university, was unthinkable. This was the elite university, the center of learning. Returning a generation later and seeing what had happened to that school in terms not just of numbers and quality but in its position in the psyche of society, I could only conclude that the institution itself has been diminished.

In fact there has been a transformation away from the idea of the autonomy of the university to its being just another public institution. The respect that was given to the university as a center of learning and the perception that the trustees had a societal responsibility and were the leaders of social movements at the same time—that whole perspective has changed.

Do we have a substitute for institutions which once had such respect and such a vital social role? If not, what are we doing in coping with that yawning gap that exists on the science side, a gap that is growing every day and is going to contribute to the further marginalization of these societies? If we do not effectively transform the mechanisms for the creation of more scientists in the South and the empowerment of scientists and intellectuals in order to achieve what needs to be achieved—if we do not transform the existing mechanisms, what then?

These are the challenges that we face. There is no question that we need reform in terms of the governance of the universities, their autonomy and independence, and their sense of accountability to the community of the university itself. *In loco parentis*, as it used to be called, needs to be reaffirmed. More than this, though, the governance of universities needs a purpose, and the sense of purpose itself has been lost.

A Possible Answer

Today I hear talk about preparing people for the market. Well, maybe. Employment is important. If that is the case, though, then universities will have been degraded to vocational schools. That is not the purpose of the university. There has to be more, a greater purpose.

It is here that I would like to suggest a slightly different nuance on this whole debate. It is that to function in tomorrow's market it will not be through the acquisition of vocational skills but through the ability to master knowledge. Thus, the need is to develop a cadre of people who can create out of a nation a "learning nation," one that can adapt to the most recent developments

in knowledge, participate in creating the knowledge, and adopt this knowledge for the society's needs.

This mastery of knowledge would be a different form of construction and educational enterprise than one that simply churns out people for employment based on the requirements of current employers in the private or the public sector.

What I am describing is a different challenge, and the mission this entails needs to be affirmed. I would say that to assert this new mission, we need to bring forth values.

Science Has Values

I may sound romantic to some of you, but I submit that I am not. The values of science are the values that we must promote in order not only to have science, but also to have a modern society. What do I mean by that? The late Jacob Bronowski expressed a great thought when he said, "Those who claim that science is value-neutral confuse the results of science, which are, with the practice of science, which is not."

In fact to practice science in a university or a research laboratory or elsewhere, we must create an atmosphere that is based on certain values. What are those values?

The first is truth. The worst thing that scientists can do is to falsify their data. It is an inexcusable transgression in the entire global scientific community.

The second value is honor. The second worst crime for a scientist is to plagiarize the work of someone else rather than recognize and honor other scientists.

Third is honoring imagination. Clearly, what is most honored about all the great advances in science is the imaginative leap that carried us to a new frontier. It is not simply the rote replication of what has already been done, but the creative breakthrough that is most valued; imagination is an essential element.

Finally, perhaps unique to science, is a certain constructive subversiveness. Why do I say that? Because the scientific paradigm is such that we advance only by replacing the current orthodoxy in such a way that it does not diminish respect and the honor for that which already exists. When Einstein's view of the world replaced Newton's, it did not diminish Newton, and Hawking's view does not diminish Einstein.

In this way of thinking, we are in the great world of Newton when he said "If I have seen further, it is because I have stood on the shoulder of giants." We are in fact honoring the past but advancing beyond. Thus, the entire scientific enterprise requires openness to the most extreme ideas, whatever they may be, however outrageous they may be, subject to a system of verification.

In this way of thinking, the youngest person can challenge the most established order. A good friend of mine was commenting earlier on the fact that so many Nobel laureates in science have made their breakthroughs when they were so young. In fact there has rarely been a breakthrough in physics that was of Nobel quality by someone who was older than forty. The practice of science, then, is not just a matter of seniority: it is a constructive subversiveness, because we know that implicit in the enterprise is the ability to change.

I submit to you that these values are not just necessary for the practice of science. They are societal values, deserving to be retained for the development of society itself.

A Key to Good Science and Good Education

In this sense, therefore, we cannot dissociate the values of science from those of society. For those interested in higher learning and science in developing countries, this has a real bearing on what can be achieved, as indicated by an empirical case I will give you: the International Laboratory for Research in Animal Diseases, based in Nairobi, Kenya, with an annual budget of seven million dollars.

ILRAD has made scientific breakthroughs such as the development of the first parasitic vaccine. Twenty percent of the worldwide effort on the mapping of the bovine genome is done there. The caliber of scientists it has attracted include Peter Doherty, who just won the Nobel Prize last year. He was, for six years, the program chair of ILRAD.

Why is it that in a developing country in Sub-Saharan Africa, for a relatively modest amount of money, you can have not just world class science, but sustained world class science being practiced at the cutting edge for fifteen years or more?

It is not the money, or the buildings, or the labs, and it is not even the people, because you can import the people, as we have seen in many of the universities in Kuwait or Saudi Arabia, where people were invited to come from all over. Rather, it has to do with the kind of atmosphere that was created in that center, where people have been intellectually challenged to do this kind of scientific work. It is not the geographic location, the size, or the population. There is something, instead, to be said about the values that govern the enterprise, the institutional culture, if you will.

I submit that unless we bring this back into the educational system, and find ways to create such centers of excellence, in terms of the freedom of inquiry that is necessary for people to do research and challenge society, we will not be able to advance.

This is the role not just of those in government, but it is also of the educators in the university system who inculcate these values into the new generation. It is a big challenge, and I regret to say that many of the educators one sees today in the universities of the developing world are not rising to this challenge. Some are people who are just banking on seniority, or on political connections, or on other criteria, and in fact cannot play that role or impart it to others.

Consequently, we may perhaps have to seek an even greater break from the status quo than would otherwise be the case, and to do that, we may have to turn to the young, as in the example of the scientific breakthroughs.

I leave you now with these lines from Robert Frost:

> Now I am old my teachers are the young.
> What can't be molded must be cracked
>   and sprung.
> I strain at lessons fit to start a suture.
> I go to school to youth to learn the future.

The Social–Natural Science Gap in Educating for Sustainable Development

Peter Thatcher

I am going to start in the late 1950s. The United States had some meteorological satellites and there was a temptation in the Eisenhower Administration to "go it alone," to follow, in effect, the Manhattan Project mold of one state with very little foreign participation to create a breakthrough, in this case, in weather forecasting.

The problem was handed over to the incoming Kennedy administration in 1961, and it became clear that there would be greater benefits for the United States if the effort were carried out internationally with collaboration, including a sharing of costs and benefits.

I had a small hand in a speech that President Kennedy made in which the United States proposed something called a world weather watch. This was in the fall of 1961, as I recall. My point here is first that the United States had a specific objective—a reliable two-week weather forecast. With the meteorological satellites, we thought we could see how to get there.

In order to get such a forecast, it was evident that there had to be an exchange of information, thinking, and ideas—real communication—between atmospheric science and ocean science, because the key was the energy exchange across the surface of the ocean. Yet, at that point there was no way for those two disciplines to communicate with each other.

An ancillary part of the United States proposal for the world weather watch was that there should be something called GARP, the Global Atmospheric Research Program. This was well-funded and was led by the World Meteorological Organization and a number of national academies and meteorological departments around the world.

Interdisciplinary Thinking

The real hidden agenda for GARP was to force useful dialogue between two disciplines that did not in the 1960s have common algorithms or common formulas, or even common models. Here was one way to achieve a multidisciplinary or interdisciplinary approach.

Years later in 1991 we had a meeting in preparation for the Earth Summit in Rio in which the International Council of Scientific Unions tried to combine with the International Social Science Council for a multidisciplinary discussion hosted by the Austrian government. The idea was to help plan what would be the science research agenda for the next century, that governments would look at in Rio in June 1992.

It was really embarrassing to sit in the room and watch as the chemists, the physicists, the biologists, and all of the related multidisciplinary, hard science, and natural science people communicated with other in a way that was unthinkable just a few decades ago and then to watch them in the audience as the economists spoke.

I am picking on the economists because we are at the World Bank. The audience was like school children laughing and giggling at each other, because they heard the hapless economists

48

using a language designed not to communicate outside their field of specialty. Anthropologists had no trouble at all in communicating, and geographers have always served as a convergence group where so-called hard science and soft science can be interrelated in socially useful ways.

The remark that was made by one person this morning was absolutely right: knowledge, perhaps including the trend of increased specialization, does force collaboration.

Now what does collaboration mean? It doesn't mean programs per se. Instead, it means process, and it means that the way that a process is designed to force different disciplines to rub shoulders is absolutely critical.

We had some success with this approach regarding the Mediterranean in the mid-1970s, when the UN Environment Programme was charged with creating what became the Mediterranean Action Plan.

In that project it proved easy to get the scientists together, as well as the fisheries people and the mayors, and then carry out a process so that the results of each of these rather specialized preparatory meetings could be played off against a different discipline, ending up with the ultimate arbiters, namely, the governments who signed the Barcelona Convention in 1976, that included research programs for the economic development of both the North and the South of the Mediterranean.

The process of collaboration, that is all the more necessary today, is critically important and can be achieved.

Participatory Approach

On another point Alvaro Umana reminded us earlier today of the need for bottom-up participation. How true it is. How silly anyone was, 30 or 40 years ago, to think of top-down world government.

Let me describe something happening in this country in which I am involved. The Environmental Protection Agency (EPA) came to the conclusion not long ago that the whole top-down regulatory approach had accomplished about all that could reasonably be expected of it in terms of clean air and clean water. Not that the top-down approach was a very efficient way to go,

but it had seemed to be the only way, given the severity of the crises being faced in this country, so they decided to try to find a way for a bottom-up approach.

In New England there are 12 so-called sole-source aquifers. Such an aquifer produces the water for more than 50 percent of the inhabitants of the watershed around it. The one that was chosen by the federal agencies as a pilot project for protection is called the Pawkatuck aquifer, serving 14 towns, 10 of them in the state of Rhode Island and four of them in Connecticut, where I live.

The purpose of this pilot effort in which several federal agencies are engaged, and, increasingly, there are stakeholders at the town level is to find out what top-down agencies can contribute to the quality of decisionmaking where it counts, at the ground level, at the local level.

A year and a half after this project began, we are trying to set up networks among elected officials; appointed town planners; tourist bureaus in Rhode Island; the Turf Growers Association— a very significant user of water—Rotary Clubs; and "tree-hugging greenies." I chair the conservation commission of the town where I live.

In this experience it is remarkable to see the degree to which federal agencies can be useful in spite of the widespread current American feeling that the federal government is not very helpful, that it really just takes money away from the taxpayers.

A Strategy the World Bank Could Follow

In short we are beginning to have some success in this New England project, and I suggest this participatory approach as something that intergovernmental agencies, particularly the World Bank, should be trying to emulate.

Interestingly, in the UN reform program now underway, the notion is to build a house in every country that the UN is trying to serve, and to let the house in that country be the focal point for information, technical assistance, the provision of knowledge, and, of course, for money. The aim is to help local people make better decisions and draw up their own strategies for sustainable development.

By the way, I believe that geographic information systems (GIS) is a valuable tool for analysis that integrates both natural science data and information, along with social science results, and I want to note that the World Bank is applying it. Just before lunch I went to see how the Bank is using this system in the region of Bangladesh, eastern India, Nepal, and Tibet. The power of a good GIS program is striking, even if it is on a portable computer, which is the way it was shown in the exhibit across the street. In that case the program integrates hydrographic data with the educational values of different districts within, for example, India.

Continuing in the vein regarding bottom-up participation and increased agency effectiveness, it seems to me as an outsider who has been critical of the Bank over the years, that promotions are given in the Bank to officers who complete a project preparation at the moment that the money becomes available to use it, and that anything that gets in the way of that timely processing of a proposed project is going to limit one's future job potential.

That is a basic problem of all the financing institutions I am familiar with. Not enough time is given, nor enough attention paid, to process, engaging different disciplines, especially thinking from the bottom up.

Can we afford to slow down in our processes in order to achieve more sustainable development in the design of national or local strategies? I do not know, but I think that what Clovis Maksoud said this morning about an interdisciplinary approach to sustainable development is absolutely unavoidable. Any organization that fails to take advantage of Dr. Serageldin's background in architecture and engineering will be criticized to the point of eventually becoming irrelevant.

Applying Collaboration to Education

In the same vein I hope that the design process for academic institutions will somehow find a more active way to involve a forced mixture of different disciplines, not necessarily within the same classroom, but as much as possible on campus, even in terms of dormitories.

I was shocked at my own university. With all of the money that Yale had, until a few years ago there were computers all over the campus but no way for medical students to talk to law students or undergraduates. I do think it has improved now.

One of the characteristics of North American academic curricula is that we have seen advanced degrees being awarded in multidisciplinary matters at the University of California in Berkeley and even at Massachusetts Institute of Technology, where chemical engineers are now talking to civil engineers who are talking to mechanical engineers and even political scientists and historians.

These are the qualities that are needed if universities are to shape students who are capable of engaging in multidisciplinary work for sustainable development. It takes a certain atmosphere—the shape of the tables and common facilities to draw students from different disciplines together—to make a big difference.

Global Ecosystem Governance and Transboundary Requirements

Claudio Grossman

I am a member of the Inter-American Commission on Human Rights at the same time that I work in a university. The commission is a 7-member body elected by the General Assembly of the Organization of American States We are now conducting hearings concerning alleged violations of human rights. The commission is a semi-judicial body. We receive petitions by citizens, or even noncitizens, and we process those, saying whether or not there have been violations of international concerns.

We see reflected in such a human rights instrument a significant and dramatic change. Imagine that only 50 years ago the way in which a government treated its own citizens was considered to be no one else's business. Now we have universally accepted norms that really constitute a yardstick to determine compliance with some values of human dignity.

Another dramatic change is that we now have supervisory mechanisms with independent experts who, as I have been describing, act in accordance with legal traditions to investigate cases and to reason and decide on the various interpretations advanced by governments and petitioners.

In the eighteenth and nineteenth centuries and the beginning of the twentieth century all of this was not possible. There were no conditions for it to happen. Independent experts who might decide whether a state was responsible for human rights violations? It just was not done.

A very interesting phenomenon now is that individuals acting at the international level as petitioners are represented by lawyers, advocates in the realm of human rights, whomever they may choose. They can even act against their government, mostly against their government, as a matter of fact. It is a very dramatic and unique situation, compared to the past where we did not have the concepts nor the instruments to check the way in which governments behaved toward their own citizens.

A Small Club of Nations

Let me provide some background so that we can better assess just how dramatic the change is, because I want to make some comments on international law and link them to the current situation and then, if time allows, share a couple of thoughts related to legal education.

First, in comparing the present with the past, classic international law is the term we use to refer to that law developed in the eighteenth century by a small club of Christian Western countries, particularly those of Western Europe.

The characteristics of this club were pretty interesting. First, it was a small group of nations. Second, the members were gentlemanly, free to do what they wanted inside their own territory. Another component was that, internally, most matters of concern could be solved by the nation state. By the way the degree of commercial interaction of any one nation with other members of the club certainly was not major.

Thus, each government had real power to do certain things inside its territory. It had sovereignty, and sovereignty was a legal term for a material reality, a reality of the power of a government to affect the life and property of its own citizens. This small club of Western Christian nations also had outside sovereignty. I do not want to get very technical, but the point is the following: The agreements of the members of the club would cease and terminate if one member decided to wage war on someone else. The attitude was "Nobody's going to tell me what I need to do, internally or externally." This small club also was free to colonize, and distinctions were made here that are still in some legal documents. If you take a look in the statute of the International Court of Justice, you will find the following phrase: "Principles of law accepted or common to civilized nations."

At that time Africans and people from the Middle East might not have been considered civilized by Western cultures. The Japanese were not considered a civilized nation in the not-too-distant past, as a matter of fact. When I read Articles 36 to 38 of the statute for the International Court of Justice, I always wonder what remains there that has legal force, because the expression, "civilized nation" is still used.

My point is that sovereignty was important. In another illustration an international court decision upheld this reasoning in the so-called Lottos case between France and Turkey in the early twentieth century. To paraphrase the court finding, countries do not have any international obligation if they did not accept it. There is no international legal responsibility without accepting it.

New Reality of International Interaction

Much time need not be spent comparing this kind of thinking with the current reality, including the tremendous changes in the nature of life in the twentieth century. We all know the economic links—trade and the requirements of production—as well as the connections through technology, now and as we move into the twenty-first

century. Interaction with others has become unavoidable.

I am certain that it has not escaped your attention that there is some universality of values. In fact we have come a long way in this regard. Now there is something known as the democratic entitlement. Some people in international law claim that if democracy is not a right, then it certainly is an entitlement, reflecting a growing consensus that democratic governance is no longer an option for everyone to choose or not to choose. Indeed there are considerations of legitimacy moving in that direction.

In the Council of Europe, for example, a country is not seen as a member if it is not a democracy. Meanwhile, the nations of this hemisphere have passed a resolution resulting in a new provision in the charter of the Organization of American States to the effect that a nondemocratic government cannot be a member of the organization and can be suspended if it is not.

We see all this change, and it indicates something very important:

> We recognize the nature of the problems facing humankind; since we are all part of the problem, we must all be part of the solution. In the past, many problems could be solved exclusively, or primarily by the single act of a state. Now there is hardly a problem that could be solved by one country alone. It is a very different situation than under classic international law.

Impacts on International Law

How has this new reality affected the law of the present? It has in 3,000 ways, many of which are difficult to quantify. First, decision-making has changed. We have moved from the Lottos case rationale—no obligation without agreement—to other types of possibilities that may create obligation. In fact it may sometimes seem that for the purposes of generating legal obligation everyone is important. As a result some lawyers are going to be totally exhausted, or we might have a war, or violations of human rights.

As a result we see that through different instruments or mechanisms, international organizations are taking an expansive view of the powers in their charter. They are coming up with interpretations allowing bodies of restricted composition to take the responsibility to produce normative instruments of different force that allow for obligations without agreement.

Article 25 of the UN charter says every member of the General Assembly is compelled to abide by the decisions of the Security Council. Somebody will say, "That is a treaty obligation." Another provision says that even nonmembers of the United Nations have to accept such decisions.

I would recommend that those who have an interest in international law read the North Sea Continental Shelf case by the International Court of Justice. The case provides another rationale for obligations arising from general treaties that have universal ratification, where such ratification does not mean everyone, but just a representative group. Thus I would suggest that we are moving away from this idea of no obligation without agreement.

We are also moving away from the idea that only states are actors. Again, this is not an ideological decision. Rather, it is a pragmatic shift reflecting the realities of contemporary life. States are no longer the only actors because we have, for instance, liberation movements and terrorist groups. Not everything is good news here in terms of transnational movement. We also have multinational corporations, which play positive roles, although there are international issues involved.

New Roles for Individuals

We see a proliferation of actors—and when I use that term, I include you and me. Individuals can now operate on the international plane in human rights and in more or less related fields. We are the objects of norms and then, through interpretation, we are creating and developing certain norms.

I will cite my own experience in the Inter-American Commission on Human Rights. We interpret human rights treaties that apply in the hemisphere and we are persuaded by arguments presented by petitioners. We see petitioners having an influence in the development of legal standards.

While the distinction between legal and political agreements was very clear in the past, that is changing. It is more a continuum because, while some political agreements might not be in force in a court of law, you can still develop expectations concerning such agreements.

So we see individuals playing a role on the international plane, and our roles change depending on the type of instrument. You have watched the debate in this country involving fast track. Treaties have gotten very cumbersome, involving many issues, and not only in the United States. Domestically, internally, there also are impacts and we develop new mechanisms allowing us more flexibility to deal with the complexities created by the situation.

State and Global Affairs: A Fuzzy Distinction

I could go on, but what I would suggest is that the distinction between internal and external matters has become fuzzy. In fact it is very difficult now to find a purely domestic issue. Article 2, paragraph 7, of the Charter of the United Nations says that nothing in the charter allows the organization to interfere in matters that belong in the domestic jurisdiction. What is domestic jurisdiction? Certainly not human rights. Certainly not peace and security. Certainly not various environmental damages.

Practically speaking, the distinction between domestic and international matters does not exist anymore, and legal education is trying to cope with this situation.

Even if the United States is in a comparatively good position in the legal realm regarding international issues, our lawyers continue to be educated in the classic mold of the nineteenth century. By contrast, we need to organize education in such a way as to promote the values we are discussing here, values which reflect that the distinction between domestic and international matters is no longer very meaningful.

Yes, it is a world that needs cooperation. We need to work together at prevention. We need early warning capacities, and we need to learn that we share a common destiny.

Discussion

Vinod Thomas: I would like to open up the discussion and invite people to comment on the issues that Claudio Grossman and Peter Thatcher have addressed.

Audience comment: I would like a little clarification on this "domestic/international" question that has been raised. Interestingly, the experience of countries such as India has been that when they have wanted the international system to intervene, they have failed to find the ways of bringing this about. I am thinking of the Bhopal case in which the matter was first brought to the American courts and dismissed on the grounds of them being an inconvenient forum, so that they then had to go back to domestic courts and domestic legislation.

The other example I am thinking of is Rwanda, where there was supposedly only limited genocide. The will to completely eliminate an ethnic group was, according to international agencies, not demonstrated. Thus, it was again assumed that the matter did not fall to the international community to intervene, at least not for a very long time.

Claudio Grossman: The domestic/international dichotomy or distinction is being increasingly challenged. For example, are matters of internal due process—in cases where someone is accused of a crime—always domestic issues? In fact we have treaties, norms of custom, and customary law that create international expectations, entitlements, and rights.

The news is not that some governments still argue that these cases are purely domestic. The news is that now this position does not have legitimacy in some situations.

For instance consider the following: We may have an accusation of genocide against a country. Somebody says, "Well, whether I kill or not, this is a domestic matter." Thus the accusation may not carry any weight. I would suggest, however, that we are in the process of moving away from that way of thinking. We are challenging it through treaties and through customs, softening the requirement of absolute agreement on such matters as obligation and responsibility.

If a state is behaving in a totally irresponsible fashion, is it possible at the current level of development of international law for that state to say, "This is only a domestic problem"? In fact we have debatable situations: the process of structuring a new reality is complex, with elements of rational decisionmaking through treaties, conferences, and agreements, and through trial, error, and practice.

Your question is very important. In no way do I want to imply that we are at the end of the road, with a clear charter that says whether or not a problem is going to be tackled by the international community. In any case, however, in terms of the World Bank and the International Monetary Fund the way in which countries conduct economic policies in the Western Hemisphere is no longer a matter of exclusively domestic jurisdiction.

Audience comment: I wish to address the science problem described earlier. I have been in all the countries of Asia and have seen the more inspired governments setting up scientific research institutes and scientifically based universities. They are capable of throwing capital at the problem, but they are not able to throw skilled humans at it.

Thus, you may see a building that looks very impressive, and you go into it and you realize that everyone you talk to, except the director, has only a bachelor's degree. They cannot do the work. There is at least a generation of learning needed. This is an area in which the developed nations can and should assist, and there are ways of doing it.

What we must remember is that more than three-quarters of all the universities in the world have been created since the Second World War. You just cannot have what was. What was is gone. We now have a multiplicity of universities, and we have learned something that is fundamentally important to humanity: that all of us are intelligent. It is not true that the world consists of very intelligent people and dummies. All humans are intelligent enough to receive benefits from higher education. Our problem is that we do not have the structures that would enable us to create a world in which universal higher education is possible.

Anyway, we should not just talk about the mission of the university. We should talk about the missions—plural—of the universities, because higher education is now such a large system that there should be diversity and there should be a multiplicity of possibilities and purposes.

Audience comment: We are talking about knowledge, and universities are those institutions that deal with the production and the sharing of this knowledge. We are talking about universities in developing countries that no longer have the basic functions to be called true universities. I am wondering what UNESCO, the institution of the UN dealing with such matters, is doing as we face this particular concern.

For instance is there a way to close the universities that no longer meet basic higher education functions, instead of allowing them to give studies that are not adequate and having people who get their degrees from those universities not be recognized as either scholars or good engineers? As it is now, we are producing people who are frustrated. They cannot get employment. Now what is the role of UNESCO with regard to this particular problem?

Audience comment: A presenter spoke in glowing terms about science. Of course we need science, but I would remind the people here that science is not a universal mode of knowledge. It is not a path to knowing all of reality.

Actually, science is a very particular mode of knowing a certain aspect of reality, quantitative reality. Its modus operandi is objectivity, which excludes subjectivity, and therefore excludes values, and, therefore, ethics. Why has education failed this lofty aim that it gave itself at one time? You can answer this with one word: materialism. We have reduced our interests to material objects, to material aims. As long as we look just at material aims, we will not be able to cope with the world's problems and provide humanity with what it needs to lift itself to a higher level of humanness.

Audience comment: I would like to focus your attention on the following: first, I would like to point to the distortions and falsifications of history and world cultures, especially by developed and Western societies, and I would like to advocate the establishment of an agency to monitor these negative effects. There may already be institutions doing this, but there is a need to have one agency to channel and centralize the results of the monitoring.

The second point is the hoarding of knowledge. The latest culprit in this respect, as was pointed out yesterday, is the intellectual property rights agreement. This is clearly a tool by the developed nations to exploit and make money out of their knowledge and advanced technologies. Therefore, I would advocate a campaign to eliminate this agreement.

Claudio Grossman: Rome was not built in a day, and it is dramatic that there has been acceptance of this mechanism. I can see a pattern of agreements that would not result in binding decisions but would provide recommendations that go to a political body. I think that is the motive. Go to the Bank's board, correct?

Of course reality does not always goes in one direction. Looking at the experience of numerous supervisory bodies, these have created situations where we move from soft political commitments to binding commitments and, in this process of establishing an authorized body that can arrive at a binding decision, there is a political price to be paid for rejecting a recommendation.

Gustavo López Ospina: In answer to the question about UNESCO and universities, everybody knows that UNESCO is an intellectual organization and that we work with governments and people on this issue of university capacity, promoting human development, and basic science.

However, we need to understand that the problem is not only the need for cooperation and solidarity. It is also a structural problem at both the global and the national levels, and, particularly, we need political support.

For example, at the national level if a government does not give priority to education, it is very difficult for UNESCO to take the responsibility. We do not have this responsibility. Today, however, with globalization, there are new possibilities for cooperating with specific regions and specific universities, and for linking up internationally. Today we have important pertinent programs, including networks for working together with the universities and governments on knowledge and information.

Knowledge, Finance, and Sustainable Development

Vinod Thomas

It is well known that societies underinvest in environmental protection and that financial investments in environmental activities remain inadequate. Policies to correct these problems are lacking, as is investment in knowledge on the environment to support these actions. Why is underinvestment so extensive?

- Damages from environmental degradation are inequitable and go beyond the present to affect future generations. These costs are seldom factored in decisionmaking by individuals who see only their own private and short term gains. Thus private returns on investment in environmental protection are significantly smaller than the benefits that accrue to society today and in the future.
- Policies (taxes, incentives, and regulations) can, in principle, correct such underinvestments in environmental protection. However, partly because of inadequate information on the causes of environmental degradation and partly because of higher priority being assigned to other activities (growth and macroeconomic stability), countries seldom take adequate policy measures to correct the neglect of the environment.
- All this is compounded by the lack of diffusion of knowledge on the environment to individuals in the public and private sectors who could press for stronger environmental actions.

Addressing underinvestment in knowledge and learning can stimulate financial investments for the environment.

This paper looks at these three types of related underinvestments—in knowledge, in policies, and in financing. We focus especially on the role of knowledge to support policies and investment opportunities for improved environmental protection. The motivation is to highlight how knowledge is being utilized by stakeholders for sustainable environmental management. Figure 1 illustrates how knowledge can be infused into NGO and civil society and into financiers, financial markets, and the public sector to promote environmentally sustainable investments.

Based on the analysis in this paper, we find that successful examples of synergy among knowledge, investments, and environmental protection may be divided into three categories:

1. Achieving "win-win" outcomes through trade or business contracts between two or among more groups
2. Improved environmental standards through a "carrot-and-stick" approach
3. New opportunities for profitable environmental investments.

We find that the public sector has been highly proactive in the collation and dissemination of knowledge across all three categories of initiatives. Not surprisingly, NGOs and the

Editor's note: This paper was prepared by Vinod Thomas, Nalin Kishor, and Tamara Belt.

Figure 1 Knowledge for environmental financing

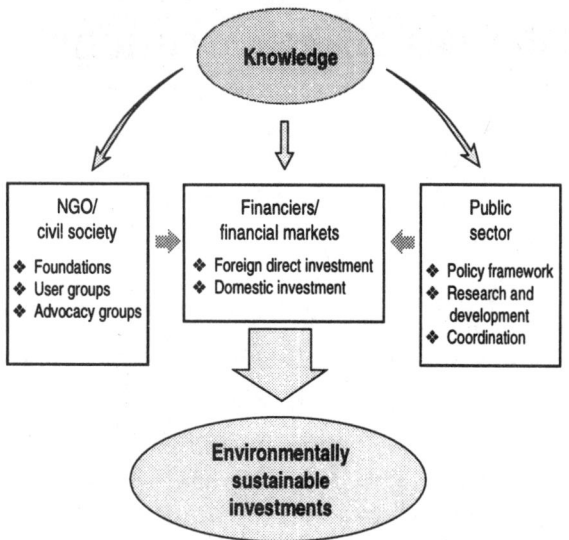

civil society have had an important role in the first two categories of activities. In these cases, the public sector and NGOs have worked together to identify investment opportunities of both the win-win and carrot-and-stick approaches. Finally, the private sector has benefited from being a recipient of knowledge (typically from the public sector), except for one instance where it directly applied basic knowledge for profitable environmental investment.

Without exception all the innovative cases for environmental management discussed in this paper owe their success to the infusion of knowledge. Such examples are occurring the marketplace in recent years, and their numbers are likely to accelerate even further, as diffusion of knowledge identifies opportunities that the private sector can exploit. Thus in the following section we focus on the potentially powerful contribution that knowledge can make to break the logjam of underinvestment in environment and encourage improved environmental policies and management.

Using the Power of Knowledge

Lasting changes in the way resources are used can only be achieved if common values and consensus among stakeholders exists for sustainability. The essence of this necessary condition is a fundamental understanding of ecological systems and their relationship with socioeconomic systems. Better knowledge management (both its production and dissemination) is critical to increase the demand for environmental quality; to improve the supply of options (policy and technology) for the management of the environment and natural resources; and to incrementally increase the financial investments necessary to address environmental sustainability. It also helps to expand the menu of choices for dealing with the environment.

Knowledge Base for Sustainability

During the past two decades of economic reforms, the accumulation of knowledge on the environment in the public and private sectors and civil society has significantly lagged behind market dynamism. In particular, an understanding of the effects of environmental damage on human and ecosystem health and its ill effects on efficiency is lacking. Knowledge of the environment tends to be amassed in crisis situations, such as oil spills, chemical contamination, cholera epidemics, nuclear meltdowns, or forest fires. Most recently, the intense environmental crisis in Southeast Asia caused by the combined effect of fires caused by humans, El Niño, and drought brought environmental damage to the international spotlight once again.

The shortcomings of this pattern of information accumulation are threefold. First, knowledge of and information on the environment becomes available only after the damage has occurred. Second, the information is only an advisory of poor environmental conditions. Third, proactive steps to immediately reverse the trend are not outlined. Eventually clean air statutes may be enacted, or forest management policies implemented, but these occur well after the damage has been done. In fact, this process of the accumulation of knowledge on the environment may explain why "grow now, clean up later" has been the conventional way to manage environmental problems in the past in both industrial and developing countries.

Increased knowledge of ecosystems and the costs of environmental damage and clean up has however shown that "grow now, clean up later" is not an effective approach to deal with environmental damage. Research on the costs of industrial pollution in Japan on human health, particularly in the cases of *Minamata and Itai-Itai* diseases and *Yokkaichi asthma*, has shown that the costs of clean up and compensation to victims are anywhere between 1.4 to 102 times the costs of prevention (Kato 1996). The investments required to clean up the Chesapeake Bay in the United States and the Danube in Europe, both of which were once highly productive natural assets, reinforce the lesson that neglecting the environment to promote growth is a costly mistake that should not be repeated by developing countries. Given that improved knowledge and data on the environment is available regarding the ecological and economic expense of the "grow now, clean up later" approach and that an ex ante approach is more cost effective than ex post, who are the most effective actors for the diffusion of knowledge?

Communicating Knowledge for Environmental Improvements

An effective way to motivate environmental financing is to change the values of people today through the effective communication of environmental issues. Complex scientific information needs to be made accessible so people can readily understand ecosystem functioning. Knowledge is embodied in people, and people (ecologists, marine biologists, environmental specialists, and sociologists) who often have the knowledge about ecosystem health and sustainability, are those who are not making management decisions or designing and implementing policy. Thus, especially in the short term, knowledge per se is not always the problem, but increasing the flow of information and thereby expanding the knowledge base to all stakeholders is the problem.

Potentially it is the public sector (national and international) that can mobilize knowledge on the environment, and link it to proactive responses in the form of policy frameworks and guidelines. For example, under the aegis of the Framework Convention on Climate Change (FCCC), a pilot phase to test joint implementation initiatives—as an approach to carbon offsets—has been approved. However, only a few parties to the convention are informed on the process of design and implementation of these projects. Thus there is a high risk that the pilot

phase may fail to yield useful results unless knowledge of technical, scientific, and economic possibilities is urgently disseminated. If increased knowledge of the convention were diffused to stakeholders, it is much more likely that binding financial agreements could be made with joint implementation projects. An example of a successful application of knowledge is discussed in the next section regarding a carbon-offset contract facilitated by the government of Costa Rica (see below Case 2: Certifiable Tradable Offsets in Costa Rica).

In addition to communicating the substance of these frameworks and conventions to encourage win-win actions, the public sectors can also draw on a wide base of knowledge from the international community, universities, and research institutions. National and local governments can use this information to influence resource use and promote cleaner environments. For example, in Indonesia the environmental protection agency (BAPEDAL), with assistance from the World Bank, has compiled information on pollution emissions from industrial firms. The agency provides local communities with this information that in turn motivates dirty firms to clean up (see below Case 5: Indonesia: A PROPER program for pollution control). In addition, the European Union has initiated a Blue Flag Campaign that disseminates environmental information to the public to raise environmental awareness and clean up their beaches in order to attract tourists (see below Case 6: The Blue Flag Campaign). In Costa Rica, the United States, and Western Europe the public sector is facilitating the dissemination and application of scientific discoveries of compounds found in biological compounds for commercial application (see below Case 7: Bioprospecting: Public-private Investments to Conserve Resources and Earn Profits). In the Maldives the government has used scientific and economic information to promote sustainable tourism (see below Case 8: Integrated Tourism Development in the Maldives).[2]

In the private sector, increased knowledge of win-win changes that benefit the producer through lower production costs and also benefit the environment through reduced consumption or degradation can have tremendous results for a cleaner environment. The major way in which these changes can be made is through the diffusion of new practices such as waste minimization in industrial processes or integrated pest control and composting in agriculture. In the United States, the Honda Motor Company itself has acted upon the information on product recycling and efficient product packaging made available by the EPA and elsewhere to streamline costs and increase its profits. However, in many cases, in order to enable sustainable investments, facilitation of the flow of knowledge to all those in the business community is critical (see below Case 1: Protection of Watersheds for Hydropower Generation, and Case 3: Exploiting the Potential of (Green) Niche markets in India).

Civil society, including NGOs, has an important role to play in encouraging sustainable development initiatives. At the policy level, by disseminating knowledge—especially to those who gain from the policy reform process—a dialogue on policy reforms can be activated and the opposition of vested interest groups can be neutralized. By infusing knowledge to all stakeholders affected by environmental degradation, the gridlock created by weaknesses in institutional capacity for monitoring and enforcement, lack of political will, and corruption can all be addressed.

NGOs have consolidated diverse pieces of knowledge and disseminated it to initiate successful environmental projects. In niche areas this has occurred in the cases of specific endangered large mammals (for example, the elephant or the white rhino). The protection of these mammals was motivated by increased information and awareness of the importance of these species for the global environment. Because of the immensely successful public campaigns organized by international NGOs, significant financing was channeled to these areas. On a local level, some unique ecosystems have been identified and recognized by local populations and governments, or both, and have been designated for in-situ protection (see below Case 4: Communal Area Management Program for Indigenous Resources [CAMPFIRE] in Zimbabwe). These areas are protected with regard to the understanding and support of the local populations. Usually this is done within the context of supportive government policy and institutions. In the case of FUNDECOR in Costa Rica, with the

diffusion of specific knowledge, the NGO was able to make a private sector energy company invest in conservation (see below Case 1: Protection of Watersheds for Hydropower Generation). In India, grassroot level NGOs have been effective in the dissemination of information to artisans on the benefits of adopting solar-powered sewing machines (see below Case 3: Exploiting the Potential of (Green) Niche Markets in India).

These examples point the way in which knowledge contributes toward improved environmental management. The dearth of knowledge and its diffusion in the past on the environment has resulted in ex post solutions to environmental issues. In order to pursue truly sustainable policies, a forward-looking vision of environmental protection, coupled with values of environmental stewardship, are needed. A fundamental way this can be motivated is through increased knowledge and diffusion on the environment.

Synergy among Knowledge, Investments, and the Environment

Increased accumulation and dissemination of knowledge to all stakeholders can turn untenable situations into opportunities for investment, increased economic efficiency, and environmental stewardship. Increased knowledge will illuminate the discussions of narrow interest groups who perceive losing by proposed changes and will facilitate changes in how the environment is managed. Many of these changes are profound and involve difficult decisions regarding property rights and resource access and use. By facilitating the flow of knowledge from those who possess to those who can support, encourage, implement, and enforce policies and mobilize investments, a cadre of environmentally aware stockholders is created and a fillip given to environmental sustainability.

The following nine cases illustrating the synergistic relationship among knowledge, investments, and environmental protection may be divided into three subcategories as follows:

1. Achieving win-win outcomes through trade or business contracts among two or more groups. Cases 1 to 4 fall into this category.

2. Improved environmental standards through a carrot-and-stick approach. Cases 5 and 6 fall into this category.
3. New opportunities for profitable environmental investments. Cases 7 to 9 fall into this category.

Opportunities in each of these categories are likely to exist in diverse countries; thus a replication and scale-up of these cases holds the promise of managing for a sustainable environment.

Case 1. Protection of Watersheds for Hydropower Generation

Global Energy is a private electric utility company that owns and operates two hydroelectric plants in the watersheds of Rio Volcan and Don Pedro in the central valley of Costa Rica. Global Energy enjoys a reputation for being an environmentally responsible company that works in close cooperation with the government.

FUNDECOR is the largest NGO in Costa Rica, with a clear mandate of preventing and reversing deforestation in the Central Valley area where these hydropower plants are located. Due to its excellent track record over the last five years, FUNDECOR has earned the respect and confidence of the government and the local landowners.

FUNDECOR approached Global Energy and, using satellite data on deforestation, was able to demonstrate to the utility that its watershed areas were threatened by deforestation. As a result, a contract was signed whereby Global Energy has agreed to pay FUNDECOR $10 per hectare per year against assured protection of its watershed areas against deforestation.

The contract is a case of a win-win situation. Through infusion of very specific knowledge, FUNDECOR succeeded in making Global Energy a willing partner in investing for environmentally sustainable development. This willingness arose largely because Global Energy could benefit from reduced risk and increased profitability. Finally, the government sees this as a start in replicating similar contracts in other parts of the country, and has already started disseminating information in this regard. This is likely to set off a virtuous spiral of environmentally sustainable investments.

Case 2. Mitigating Global Climate Change: Certifiable Tradable Offsets in Costa Rica

Under the pilot phase of the joint implementation program, industrialized countries are collaborating with developing countries to identify the cheapest options for the control of greenhouse gases. Costa Rica has designed an instrument that can be used to sell greenhouse gas offsets in the international marketplace, called the Certifiable Tradable Offset, or CTO. A CTO represents a specific number of units of carbon dioxide gas emissions expressed in carbon equivalent units reduced or sequestered through, for example, tree planting. The quality of the CTO is ensured through independent verification and monitoring by a private sector company (Castro, Tattenbach, Olson 1997).

In July 1996 Costa Rica sold its first batch of CTOs. The governments of Costa Rica and Norway, along with private sector companies from both countries, agreed to cooperate on a JI project that involves, among other things, reforestation and forest conservation. The Norwegian parties are contributing US$2,000,000 to the Private Forestry Project: US$1.7 million from the Norwegian government, financed by a Norwegian carbon tax, and US$300,000 from Consorcio Noruego (a consortium of three private sector Norwegian companies) in exchange for 200,000 CTOs.

The direct benefits of this scheme are twofold. Costa Rica received additional funds for protecting its forests and expanding reforestation. Norwegian companies receive CTOs that could be used to cheaply offset its carbon emissions in the event the greenhouse gas emissions quotas become binding.

By tapping the climate change knowledge base (FCCC and IPCC, that lays out the scientific evidence; and the framework and guidelines for international cooperation, IPCC 1996) and investing significant amounts of resources in research and development, the government of Costa Rica was able to develop this scheme. From the other side, the Norwegian government invested US$1.7 million to encourage private sector confidence and investment in the scheme. With this success, Costa Rica is now actively seeking to enter into partnerships with other countries, with a view to making CTOs into a fully marketable commodity with the potential to be traded on commodity boards worldwide. Considerable progress has already been made in this direction.

*Case 3. Exploiting the Potential
of (Green) Niche Markets in India*

The solar sewing machine conversion kit of the Green Electrons Eliminating Poverty (GEEP) retrofits a conventional pedal sewing machine to run on solar power. A shirt made on this machine has a logo to identify that it is an environmentally friendly (green) product. This is sold in niche markets for such products where it commands a higher price relative to its non-green counterpart (Gay 1997).

In order to promote adoption, garment retailers have collaborated with the conversion-kit manufacturer to provide easy credit. The government has aided retailers in the identification and development of niche markets for garments, while NGOs have been instrumental in disseminating information on the benefits of adoption of the solar-powered sewing machine to rural artisans.

This scheme generates several benefits. For the tailor, the benefits accrue in the form of increased productivity (this can double from 9 to 18 shirts a day), assured income, and onsite work. Secondary benefits linked to packaging and transportation will also accrue at the village level. For the retailer, there is the attraction of additional income through exploiting new markets and developing a green image that could translate into more profits if environmentally conscious consumers switch to this company. Environmental benefits come in the form of reduced emissions of polluting gases, had these goods been produced with fossil fuel energy.

*Case 4. Communal Area Management
Program for Indigenous Resources
(CAMPFIRE) in Zimbabwe*

The CAMPFIRE program in Zimbabwe was launched by the government in close consultation with local users of natural resources and technical experts, with the aim to more effectively manage wild species and natural resources to contribute to sustainable rural development (Muir-Leresche 1996). Rural communities that

demonstrate a capacity for sustainable wildlife management are granted legal authority to manage natural resources on their communal lands. The committees—in conjunction with technical assistance from the government and NGOs—decide how best to use wild species to contribute to rural development.

Most communities opt for a combination of ways to use their wildlife, depending on local environmental and economic conditions. Controlled safari hunting is currently the most profitable option. Other options include wildlife tourism and marketing of natural products such as hides, meat, and wood that are harvested on a sustainable basis. Revenues generated from these natural resources have contributed to community development projects such as the construction of schools, clinics, and roads, and installing wells and grinding mills. Revenues are also used to compensate villagers for livestock lost due to damage by wildlife (description of programs, Africa Resources Trust).

The reason this scheme has been successful is because it has been strongly supported by national government policy in consultation with local governments or communities. Knowledge from technical experts and indigenous local communities has guided the management decisions and has resulted in the sharing of risks of wildlife preservation between the government and local communities. Because revenues are shared between the national government and user groups, monitoring and enforcement are reduced to a minimum. Finally, initial financing was obtained from the government, NGOs (especially international NGOs), and local communities. Revenues in the medium and long term derive from tourists and from sales of natural products.

*Case 5. Indonesia: A PROPER Program
for Pollution Control*

The Program for Pollution Control, Evaluation and Rating (PROPER) in Indonesia targets pollution reduction by publicly disclosing pollution information (Wheeler and Afsah 1996). The government, in an effort to clean up polluting industries, compiled information for 187 highly polluting factories and then ranked companies on the level of emissions. Highly polluting firms were given six months to clean up: otherwise their pollution emissions would be disclosed publicly.

Through government policy and increased environmental awareness, polluting industries were forced to clean up. The compilation of information was conducted with the technical assistance of the World Bank and illustrates how information dissemination by the public sector to civil society can effectively mobilize the private sector to move toward more sustainable production patterns. In this case the monitoring and enforcement is shared by the government and civil society. Financing of the policy was conducted mainly by the government of Indonesia with financial and technical assistance from the multilateral development banks. Financing for clean-up, of course, rests with the private sector.

Case 6. The Blue Flag Campaign, European Community

The European Blue Flag Campaign is operated through a network of national organizations and coordinated by the Foundation for Environmental Education in Europe (World Bank 1993). Its main objective is to encourage citizen understanding and appreciation of the coastal environment and the incorporation of environmental concerns in the decisionmaking of coastal authorities. The EC has been financing about 25 percent of the campaign's budget (presently over ECU 1 million) and the rest by private sponsors.

A beach or marina has to meet three sets of criteria to receive the blue flag. The first tests the environmental quality of the locality. The second considers management and safety. The third emphasizes environmental education and information, that ensures that visitors are provided with environmental information on the coastal environment.

Based on a completed questionnaire, maps, photographs, and water samples, a national jury selects sites to be presented to a European jury that makes the final selection by unanimous vote. The results are announced in the beginning of June before the main holiday season. The campaign has attracted several commercial sponsors in addition to schoolchildren and other citizens.

Over the years the standards of environmental quality have been raised to provide dynamic incentives for improved environmental management.

The governments see this as an efficient way to promote environmental awareness and also increase revenues through increased domestic and foreign tourists. Private sponsors see this as an opportunity to attract more tourists through the Blue Flag award.

Case 7. Bioprospecting: Public-Private Investments to Conserve Resources and Earn Profits

Governments are beginning to understand the economic potential of local natural resources and biodiversity. The United States and many countries in Western Europe are offering tax breaks, grants, and regulatory reforms to attract private sector firms such as pharmaceuticals to invest in bioprospecting. For example, in Germany recently US$86.6 million in grants was awarded in three regions for use as biotech seed money (*Time* 1997). These awards build on local expertise and knowledge found in public universities and pave the way for the creation of new industries. For the last 35 years the US National Cancer Institute has supported a program that has searched the Earth's biodiversity for chemical structure that might have utility. A similar example is found in Costa Rica with the creation of INBio (National Biodiversity Institute), a public agency that partners with private enterprises, most notably Merck Sharp and Dohme, in addition to research institutes to explore and develop commercial applications of compounds found in the biodiversity contained in the rainforests (Figueres 1997).

Critical to the success of all these initiatives are the incentives from the state to bear some of the risks for venture capitalists and at the same time support research and development to increase the knowledge base on the environment. There is also a visible change of thinking among European academics who are beginning to feel less inhibited about turning cutting-edge research into corporate profits, in the name of the environment. These actions in turn are fueling investments. According to the European Venture Capital Association, its members invested nearly

$160 million in biotech firms last year, an increase of 53 percent over 1995.

Case 8. Integrated Tourism Development in the Maldives

Coastal tourism is difficult to manage in developing countries and is typically characterized by spontaneous development and clearing of coastal forest and mangroves, leading to coastal and soil erosion. Other common environmental problems associated with coastal tourism is the lowering of the groundwater table, resulting in inflows of saltwater as fresh water is pumped out; improper solid waste disposal sites; and littering.

Proactive government policy in Maldives that targets foreign direct investment in the tourism industry has resulted in favorable economic and environmental outcomes. After the first thorough evaluation of tourism in Maldives took place in 1983 ten years after tourism development, specific policy actions were made to curb spontaneous settlements. In conjunction with scientific information and economic data, government planners designed an integrated tourism plan. Strict government regulations were enacted that gave a clear signal to foreign direct investment of the viability of short and long term returns on their investments. This actions were undertaken together with fiscal and monetary adjustments to achieve macroeconomic stability in the economy.

The result was a boom in the tourism industry. Tourism in 1995 contributed 17 percent of the GDP, over 25 percent of government revenue, and 60 percent of the country's foreign exchange earnings. It is the second largest contributor to the economy and is increasing in importance every year (Saeed 1997).

Case 9. Sustainable Mariculture

SeaPhix, LLC., associated with the marine aquarium industry, aims to preserve coral reefs through the propagation of coral reefs and ornamental sea life, instead of harvesting coral reefs for exotic fish species for sale on the market. The company markets the equipment, (for example, insulated larval rearing tanks and daylight spectrum lights) and mariculture installations for the propagation of ornamental marine life based on a total ecosystem approach for the classroom or private residences. The first installations were in Tennessee and Indiana.

This company is building on a forward-looking vision of marine biodiversity preservation by moving away from teaching approaches where children are encouraged to capture a species such as exotic fish and place it in an aquarium, only to have it die months later. Now the company is using advanced scientific methods and heightened awareness of the destruction of coral reefs to encourage the propagation of coral reefs for the enjoyment of children. Exposure to the reef and other marine ecosystems in the classroom or in private homes may increase future generations' sensitivity to and need for the protection of the world' reefs (Walch 1995).

The driving forces in this example is building on increased public awareness and knowledge of the need for preservation of coral reefs. With that as a basis, the financing is solely driven by the private sector.

Findings and Recommendations

The above examples show that the traditional roles of private and public sectors are evolving in new areas and much is being left to the workings of the market. Table 1 draws out the main lessons from the above examples. It illustrates the extent to which three key agents—the public sector (international and national), the private sector, and civil society (including NGOs)—can become involved in activities to protect and manage natural resources. Three basic factors are necessary for these activities to succeed: knowledge about the opportunities; financing; monitoring and enforcement; and (enabling) environmental policy.

On the basis of the information in table 1 some of the important emerging lessons are:

• The role of knowledge in inducing environmental investments is critical in all cases. Thus FUNDECOR disseminated information on the threat of deforestation to Global Energy; and knowledge of scientific research was applied for the propagation of coral reefs for commercial profits.

Table 1 Characteristics of successful environmental investments

Success factors for environmental activities	Contributions to success factors by agents potentially involved in environmentally sustainable activities			
	Public sector (international)	Public sector/ government (national)	Private sector	Civil society and NGOs
1. Knowledge management	At the international level dissemination of knowledge (by FCCC and IPCC) is critical to the success of the CTOs in Costa Rica, and of the Blue Flag Campaign of the EU. At the national level the public sector has played a key role in disseminating knowledge for controlling industrial pollution in Indonesia, CTO scheme in Costa Rica, developing a green niche market in India, communal management of indigenous resources in Zimbabwe, bioprospecting in the United States and Europe, and tourism development in the Maldives.		In the examples considered, the private sector has not been active in dissemination but has benefited from being a recipient of information, with the exception of sustainable mariculture in the Caribbean.	Highly specific knowledge disseminated by the NGO FUNDECOR resulted in an agreement with the hydropower company in Costa Rica. In Zimbabwe, active contributions to the knowledge base by the NGOs and civil society enabled implementation of CAMPFIRE.
2. Sources of financing	No involvement in these case examples (but note role of GEF).	The government of Norway invested as a one-time inducement to the private sector to buy CTOs in Costa Rica. The government provided initial seed money in Zimbabwe and for bioprospecting in Costa Rica.	Except in the case of CAMPFIRE in Zimbabwe, private sector financing has been a characteristic feature of all these case examples.	The local communities and NGOs contribute to financing for CAMPFIRE in Zimbabwe.
3. (a) Monitoring and enforcement	No significant contributions in this area.	With the exception of hydropower in Costa Rica, governments have a pivotal role in monitoring and enforcement in all cases.	In the example of Costa Rica CTOs a private sector company has been contracted for monitoring and enforcement.	In Costa Rica hydropower an NGO will undertake monitoring and enforcement. In Indonesia civil society is involved. In Zimbabwe both NGOs and local communities are responsible. In India NGOs will monitor for green labelling.
(b) Environmental policy and laws	Significant contributions in the case of CTOs in Costa Rica.	Governments have been primarily responsible for the design and implementation of enabling policy.	Not much involvement in development of policies and laws.	In Zimbabwe NGOs and local communities have collaborated with the government on the legal and policy aspects of CAMPFIRE.

- Knowledge has been disseminated primarily by the public sector. However, in some instances knowledge has been disseminated by NGOs and civil society.
- The private sector emerges as the predominant player in financing environmental investments. In two cases (CTOs in Costa Rica and CAMPFIRE in Zimbabwe) the public sector has provided finance, but only as a one-time inducement.
- Monitoring and enforcement is not only the responsibility of the public sector. Increasingly, the civil society and NGOs can assist in this, and are often more effective and may indeed be critical (for example, pollution control in Indonesia) to ensuring the desired outcomes.

Two additional lessons that emerge from the case examples and the discussions in this paper more generally are:

- Typically, highly specific learning and information is necessary and sufficient to spark off the investment, such as occurred with the hydropower in Costa Rica. However, in some cases a holistic approach comprising of dissemination of knowledge, technological innovations, policy, credit, and product market development is required to induce investments (for example, the green niche market in India).
- The role of the public sector to establish a framework of policies and property rights that can attract the interest of the private sector is becoming increasingly important. The international public sector is responsible for setting global framework and convention guidelines. Governments are the primary agents that can implement these guidelines into policy. In all instances knowledge helps formulate more effective policies.

Concluding Remarks

First, in the area of environmental policy reforms, we have already seen how diffusion of knowledge can contribute to achieving consensus between diverse stakeholders on the one hand, and neutralize the opposition of narrow interest groups, on the other. The result is positive both in the better design of policies and in their effective implementation.

Next, in the case of investment flows, the main focus of this paper, we have seen how the infusion of knowledge has often provided a sufficient spark for financing for the environment. Based on the case examples presented in this paper, it is found that the public sector is strategically placed for the building and the diffusion of knowledge and establishing policy frameworks that encourage environmentally sustainable investments. The private sector has a comparative advantage for financing environmental activities, because it is most closely linked to financial markets. Finally, NGOs and the civil society have a critical role in knowledge diffusion to the public in order to build up a multistakeholder consensus on environmental issues; and also to private companies with regard to motivating and monitoring cleaner business practices.

It is clear that the most innovative cases for environmental management have arisen due to the infusion of knowledge by the public and private sectors and civil society. Such examples will increasingly proliferate the marketplace, as the diffusion of knowledge identifies opportunities that the private sector can exploit. Thus, if these examples can be scaled up and rolled out, prospects for a sustainable environment would look much brighter. Knowledge management is likely to be a powerful tool to improve environmental management.

Notes

1. Without implicating them, we would like to acknowledge the helpful comments received from Wilfrido Cruz, Mansoor Dailami, Farrukh Iqbal, Mohan Munasinghe, and Yan Wang.

2. Other innovative examples include U.S. President Bill Clinton's recent educational event on global warming for weather forecasters in the hope that during weather forecasts, they would be able to influence public thinking about global warming (*The New York Times*, October 3, 1997). In Sweden, where the military draft is compulsory, education on environmental issues is integral to the curriculum for military recruits (personal communication).

Bibliography

Castro, René, F. Tattenbach, and N. Olson. 1997. "The Costa Rican Experience with Market Instruments to Mitigate Climate Change and Conserve Biodiversity." Paper prepared for Global Knowledge '97 Conference, Toronto, Canada, June 22–25, 1997.

Figueres, José Maria. 1997. "Political Dimensions of Rural Well-Being and How to Achieve Results on the Ground." In Ismail Serageldin and David Steeds, eds., *Rural Well-Being: From Vision to Action*. Washington, D.C.: World Bank.

Gay, Charles F. 1997. "Private Sector Village Enterprise: A New Approach to Sustainable Financing." Paper presented at Village Power '97 Conference, Arlington, Va., April 14–15, 1997.

Intergovernmental Panel on Climate Change (IPCC). 1996. *Climate Change 1995: The Science of Climate Change.* Cambridge, U.K.: Cambridge University Press.

Kato, Kazu. 1996. "Grow Now, Clean up Later? The Case of Japan." In Ismail Serageldin and Alfredo Sfeir-Younis, eds., *Effective Financing of Environmentally Sustainable Development*. Proceedings of the Third Annual World Bank Conference on Environmentally Sustainable Development. Washington, D.C.: World Bank.

Muir-Leresche, Kay. 1996. "Economic Policy and Natural Resources: The Case of Wildlife in Zimbabwe." Paper presented at Promoting Growth with Equity and Environmental Sustainability, A Program of Seminars for Southern Africa, Harare, Zimbabwe. November 19-22, 1996.

Saeed, Simad. 1997. "Environmental Impact Management in the Tourism Industry of Maldives." Paper presented at the EDI/World Bank/SAARC Seminar on Economic Globalisation and Environmental Sustainability in South Asia, June 2–6, 1997.

Schmidheiny, Stephan, and F. Zorraquin. 1996. *Financing Change*. Cambridge, Mass.: The MIT Press.

Thomas, Vinod, and T. Belt. 1997. "Growth and the Environment: Allies or Foes?" *Finance & Development* (June): 22–24.

Time. 1997. "The New Icelandic Saga." (September 29): 62–63.

Walch, John. 1995. "Opportunities in Sustainable Mariculture" In Anthony J. Hooten and Marea E. Hatziolos, eds., *Financing Mechanisms for Coral Reef Conservation*. Washington, D.C.: World Bank.

Wheeler, David, and S. Afsah. 1996. *Going Public on Polluters in Indonesia: BAPEDAL's PROPER-PROKASIH Program*. Washington, D.C.: International Executive Reports.

World Bank. 1993. "Worldwide Best Practices: Innovative Environmental Management for Brazil." Environment and Agriculture Operations Division, Country Department LA1. Latin America and the Caribbean Regional Office, World Bank, Washington, D.C.

Knowledge, Finance, and Sustainable Development

Theodore Panayotou

My experience comes from trying to teach as well as to practice sustainable development, as well as doing research on it and advising governments around the world on the subject. My main job is doing research in sustainability.

Recently, I was at the White House Conference on Global Warming called by U.S. President Clinton, along with scientists, economists, and private sector environmental CEOs to think about what the United States' position on global warming should be.

Despite the persisting uncertainties, science is the easiest part. The second easiest, although quite a bit more difficult, is the economics. Clearly, the most difficult is the politics of it.

Today I read a commentary in the *Boston Globe* by Ellen Goodman. She asked several questions that are very representative of the political challenge. First she asked, "How do you get Americans to buy a policy for tomorrow, when it may cost money today?" Second she asked, "Can a country with a short attention span focus on the long run?" Her third question was, "What do you do when all politics are local and warming is global?"

These questions summarize the problems we have with sustainable development. Knowledge and finance are central to resolving these problems. How do knowledge and sustainable development relate?

Under this heading there is the matter of the kind of knowledge we need for the understanding and practice of sustainable development. There is also the kind of knowledge that we need for obtaining the necessary financing for sustainable development.

Defining Sustainable Development

My definition of sustainable development is development that does not undermine its own foundations but actually strengthens them. Sustainable development has a couple of characteristics that we are not used to in regular scientific pursuit. First, we believe in the independence of disciplines—sustainable development is intrinsically interdisciplinary and holistic.

Second, in regular subjects, we focus on issues that are more tractable, and not laden with value judgments. However, in sustainable development, we cannot escape issues of complexity as well as equity, both contemporary and intergenerational. For example, sustainable development addresses the question of how to get economies to simultaneously deal with both efficiency and equity, a complex issue laden with value judgments.

Another point is that sustainable development is not simply long-term in character—it is a super long-term issue. Think of global warming or of biodiversity. If we apply any reasonable rate of time reference, any reasonable rate of discount, however we adjust it for social considerations, global warming a couple of hundred years from now counts for little more than zero. The world's

GNP, discounted at 5 percent, 200 years from now is worth less than this building.

Meanwhile, the tools that we have developed are meant to address the short- to medium-term, or maybe some long-term problems, but certainly not the super-long, the content of which are of catastrophic proportions.

Another very important issue is that sustainable development is interactive. Its most significant area is not in the individual components but in the interactions, whether we are talking about the science, or the interactions amongst species, or the interactions of different ecosystems. Furthermore, whether we are even talking in economic or political terms, interactions are the critical reality. In contrast, those of us in "regular" science usually like to focus on items individually, assuming away interdependence.

Here we have some important analytical issues to address in the area of knowledge. As I mentioned before, knowledge is not our only need to achieve sustainable development. The picture is complicated still further by the fact that knowledge, in and of itself, may not be the binding constraint to action. Indeed, much of the knowledge that already exists is presently being disseminated in a way that it can be internalized, if not by the general public, at least by policymakers and other decisionmakers.

I would add that if we expect politicians to respond to wise public perceptions and public demands, then we want the knowledge to penetrate and be internalized down to the citizen level. There is presently a big gap between the existing knowledge and what has been internalized by the citizens. Below this level there is another gap, which is between what has been internalized and what has been put into action. While it would be unreasonable to expect to close these gaps entirely, their narrowing is just as important as the generation of new knowledge.

Let me move to the issues of financing, and I will then conclude with some changes, or new areas, on which different disciplines need to focus.

Addressing Finance Problems

One problem with the financing area is that estimates of how much is needed to put the world economy on a sustainable development path, in-

cluding estimates by the UN Conference on Environment and Development in Rio, are based on a "business as usual" scenario.

That scenario includes a huge number of distortions—subsidies for energy, water, agriculture, transport, and deforestation; all kinds of barriers to sustainable development.

We should not be estimating how much it takes to air condition this room while the heat is running at full blast, and complain that it is too expensive. We must first turn off the heat, and then estimate how much it will cost to air condition. It might cost much less than under a business-as-usual scenario; air conditioning may not even be necessary after the heat is turned off.

Unfortunately, all the estimates of financing needs of sustainable development that I have seen are based on a business-as-usual scenario, and they come up with figures on the order of half a trillion dollars a year or more.

Instead we should first try to remove subsidies for environmental degradation. Then we should try to change people's behavior by providing them with an improved incentive structure.

The other reality we need to deal with is the misdeployment of funds. No matter how much money we are able to mobilize for sustainable development, it will not make a dent in the problem if we continue to make huge investments in "bad" projects in the "wrong" sectors, and our investments have significant environmental impacts that could be easily and cheaply avoided, but are not.

Redeploying Investments

Sustainable development calls for a significant redeployment of investment funds. For instance, we have tremendous and, in the case of many developing countries, increasing resources being allocated toward military purposes around the world. If 10 percent, or even 2 percent, of that were reallocated to the education of the poor in developing countries, there would be a tremendous impact on sustainable development in terms of their empowerment, their increased economic capacity, the reduction of fertility, the improvement of nutrition, and the education of children.

Another example: we spend billions of dollars on building new infrastructure while the existing infrastructure is falling apart, but we are not providing sufficient money to maintain and efficiently operate existing infrastructure.

A Canadian study showed that it would be possible to obtain water supply and electricity through demand management at one-fifth the cost of additional expansion of the supply system. What do we do? We choose expansion. Maybe one of the problems here is not so much economists, but engineers. In fact we are all blameworthy.

The best financing method for sustainable development is a mechanism that neither raises nor spends a single dollar. The most sustainable and effective answer is the approach that motivates people to change the way they do things.

Certainly, if we have to spend money directly, we must try to find ways to minimize costs. If we do this and still achieve the same objective, we can accomplish more with the same level of resources.

People are not sufficiently comprehending the idea of using market-based instruments, community, informal regulations, and voluntary agreements to advance sustainable development. Most people see the market as the enemy to be subdued and the civil society as too weak; or they see the broader kind of approach where the communities apply pressure to get things done. We need much more education both in designing better incentive systems and in helping people. Otherwise, the market-based approaches are not likely to be adopted. Understand them and use them. Indeed, all must participate in the design and implementation of such systems.

Service-Oriented Government

Another issue I want to emphasize is that with the exception of some federalist countries and countries making serious efforts to decentralize, most of the developing world has extremely centralized administrative structures and governments.

To succeed, sustainable development requires financing and decentralization, devolution to the local level—devolution of taxing authority, of governing, and of expenditures. Without this, costly top-down decisions that are unresponsive to individual needs at the local level would prevail.

Sustainable development requires that the process of governance be oriented toward service, that is, toward serving people's needs. We should have public servants who are less focused on financing, managing operations, and supplying goods and services, and more focused on regulating, facilitating, and creating incentive structures as well as proper rules of the game.

We have not done enough to promote the private sector's participation in sustainable development. With the kind of flows that Dr. Vinod Thomas presented to us, if we ignore the private sector and its role in sustainable—or unsustainable—development, trying to increase sustainable development through public expenditures alone is a losing game. We must redirect this tremendous and increasing private capital flow toward more sustainable activities.

Comments on the Disciplines

The following are some suggestions as to how different disciplines, including my own, can promote change.

1. In the area of law we need to have a legal basis for private sector involvement in what have traditionally been public sector monopolies, such as the supply of electricity and water.
2. We need to establish a truly competitive bidding process and the drafting of fairly complete contracts with the necessary independent regulatory mechanisms. Otherwise, while this business of privatization may sound exciting, when implemented it does not work for sustainable development: it works for something else.
3. We also need more work on environmental legislation so that it is effective, enforceable, and transparent, and also provides freedom and flexibility for private industry and whomever else is being regulated to achieve environmental objectives at minimal cost. Most of the regulatory systems now in place are sanctions and punishment-oriented, rather than systems that provide incentives to change behavior.

With regard to governance, as mentioned earlier, we need more work on the decentralization and devolution of authority to local levels. More work is needed on the transparency and predictability of policy and on getting leaner but tougher, perhaps bolder, governments. Certainly, we need tougher governments that hold the private sector accountable but at the same time give the private sector the flexibility and the instruments necessary to provide efficient public service.

In the area of economics we need to pay more attention to externalities, including environmental externalities, and to intergenerational and contemporary equity. More attention is needed to ecological thresholds and how they affect our economic models. We need to focus more on the super-long run and find ways to deal with it other than by simply saying, "use social discount rate." We need more emphasis on the matter of uncertainty, and we need to focus on substitution limits, especially in the short run.

In the cases of sociology and anthropology we need to pay more attention to making the participation of stakeholders effective, authenticating national policies at the local level, revitalizing communal systems of management, and increasing people's willingness to pay for environmental protection.

In science we need more attention to interactions among different species, environments, and ecosystems and more emphasis on evolutionary biology, rather than just focusing on molecular biology.

In education emphasis is needed on a change of values from the current, consumption-oriented lifestyles to more environmentally conscious values. We need more education in business ethics, and finally, and very importantly, as mentioned in the paper by Dr. Thomas, there is a need to transfer best practices from one country to the other—that does not only mean from North to South, but also, especially, from South to South. There are a lot of win-win best practices that could be transferred, but are not. Costa Rica is doing wonderful things, but other Latin American countries have never heard about them.

To conclude, knowledge and financing are central to sustainable development, but how they are generated and deployed is far more important than their absolute levels in bringing about change on the ground. True knowledge, effectively applied, is the best substitute for limited financial resources. Without knowledge an abundance of finance may do more harm than good to the cause of sustainable development. It is the synergy between intelligently applied knowledge and judiciously deployed incentives and financial resources that holds the greatest promise that sustainable development will be translated from a slogan into reality.

Discussion

Audience comment: This is my first experience speaking at the World Bank, and I appreciate the chance to comment. My name is Nicolai Malshev, and I am from East Kazakhstan. I am the head of the Economic and Management Department of East Kazakhstan Technical University, and the director of a regional center for Junior Achievement, a nongovernmental, nonprofit educational organization.

We are isolated from all the problems of the organization of knowledge being discussed in this room, and it is a pity that in this event there are no representatives speaking from former Soviet Union countries.

Our region is open for collaboration. Are you interested in an expansion of our ideas on organizing knowledge for the environment? In the former Soviet Union we will be glad to collaborate with you. I hope to meet somebody from this auditorium in East Kazakhstan. Thank you.

Audience comment: I have just a few comments. Much of what you have said, Professor Panayotou, can be read in many documents and information papers, but we have to admit that nothing has really changed during the five years since the Rio summit. I do not really know why. Maybe the world is so complex that making new decisions and taking new directions requires a lot of time.

This is to suggest that there could be a problem with the term "sustainable development." Maybe we have to make an analysis of these two words and change them for a new paradigm, that could be "sustainable human development," or "sustainable future." In any case there is clearly a problem with the term. It is difficult for people to understand what they mean. We have to spend time explaining what is behind them.

Theodore Panayotou: My hypothesis is that we fell behind after Rio because there are some issues that we have not addressed properly. For example, economics is just starting to take into account problems such as the irreversibility of crossing ecological thresholds. Or take science, for instance. For the past three weeks I have been trying to find solid information on the fires in Indonesia—where they are, who caused them, how much of the peat forest is burning. I have sought such supposedly basic information as the location and the extent of the fires. We have called Europe, Indonesia, everywhere, yet despite all of the modern super-technologies, we could not get that information.

In fact we are being told now we may not learn what we are asking about the fires for another six months. We are not much better than Nero sitting there and playing his fiddle while Rome burned.

Here science obviously has not been keeping up with its job, because we had another fire in Indonesia 15 years ago that burned something like three or four million hectares of forest. Despite that major case, we still have not done our homework in order to have a quicker response, both in terms of information, such as available satellite images, and in terms of policy responses.

What is the consequence? We have to sit now and watch the fires burn, with tens of thousands of people suffering, affected by respiratory and other problems. Meanwhile, airports are closed, ships and planes crash, and people are killed. Have we done anything? No, because we do not have either the science or the proper public awareness about the issue. If we made a public survey, I would bet that even in the United States, 95 percent of the people have not even heard about the fires.

Furthermore, if there is this tremendous lack of knowledge in some critical matters, we have a lot of other knowledge that may not even be needed. The knowledge that we do have has a hard time percolating down to the policymakers, the local decisionmakers, and individual citizens.

Audience comment: I would just like to comment that two weeks ago the grid facility at Sioux Falls, a U.N. Environment Programme facility in South Dakota, put on the Web a detailed analysis of the precise location and specific fires that were then burning in Sumatra. This was downloaded by several thousand people.

My problem with economists generally is that they are not all like Professor Panayotou. If economics was being taught in the same way that he presented, progress on sustainable development would be a great deal better. We must better disseminate the information that is available.

Concerning engineers, there is the World Engineering Partnership for Sustainable Development, a large group of engineers who banded together a year before Rio to try to incorporate concepts of sustainability in their practice of engineering. There are codes of conduct today that are really quite superior.

Audience comment: A brief comment: first, please know that 2,000 economists, including six Nobel laureates, have signed a letter regarding the global warming issue. Second, regarding the Indonesian fires, if you really want information,

I was just there. I spent this morning on the phone with Indonesian policymakers from the Ministries of Forestry and Environment. I have talked with satellite information sources, and they do not yet have the precise figures on the fires: between 60,000 and 600,000 hectares are burning.

Audience comment: From a Cambridge University source I hear two million hectares.

Audience comment: Some of these things seem to come together. Among other matters there were comments about education. He cited imagination, honor, truth, and responsibility as necessary characteristics, but I would like to add passion, and to suggest that the passion with which Dr. Serageldin and Dr. Panayotou spoke were excellent examples of it.

We are not working together, and we are so afraid of hurting each other. Look at Darwin by comparison. He lost his health because of his scientific passion. Look at Galileo—he almost lost his life; he certainly lost his job. There are others who lost their heads. Let us lose a few heads. The Bank has to be a little more open to new ideas.

Let me make one more point. The Africans whom I have trained—and I have trained Africans for 20 years—have been socialized by a system of education in the universities in Africa, France, and North America so that they do not dare speak passionately about anything in class. The moment they get out of class, though, they say what they feel.

I am very concerned about this. The Africans have been told, "No, no, in science you have to be dispassionate." That's baloney. Science is a passion; it is love of knowledge. We have got to convert ourselves. Otherwise, there is no sustainability at all.

Vinod Thomas: I would like to close the session on this high note of passion that we all would share, including the president of this Bank. You will be seeing change reflected in many, many ways in the Bank as we go forward.

How to Proceed—How to Connect?

Saad Eddin Ibrahim

The amount of knowledge regarding the environment and sustainable development that has accumulated in this one-week conference is tremendous.

I have been coming here for the last several years since Dr. Serageldin started this tradition of an annual ESSD meeting, and every year I learn a lot. The only problem is that I do not absorb enough.

This brings us head to head with the title of our meeting: Organizing Knowledge. What do we do with all this knowledge? How do we organize and use it? Thus the last session today— "How to Proceed—How to Connect?"

I have really reflected on this question, and I do not want to make this presentation one more knowledge bombardment. I will be concentrating on answering the question *"How?"* something that academics sometimes do not concern themselves enough about, although engineers do.

The Hard Task of Changing Behavior

Let me relate two stories. One took place the first time I came here. My son was studying as an undergraduate in a university in America. He came to visit me here in Washington and he attended some of the sessions of the conference that year. He listened to Ismail Serageldin giving passionate, inspiring speeches.

As a result of that one experience of attending two or three sessions at the conference and of listening to Ismail Serageldin, my son decided to change his college major. He was studying civil engineering at the time, and he decided to change to environmental engineering, a new major in his university. The change required that he stay one more year over his regular program, and it meant $50,000 more for me. That was a lesson that I should not invite any member of my family to come and listen to Serageldin.

Now the interesting thing about my son—and I am sorry to talk about him but his is a helpful case for this particular theme—is that after he finished his engineering he did a little bit of training here, and then he was invited to work for one of the corporations in Egypt, an oil company that started an environmental division.

Very quickly he became the deputy chief of that division, and part of his work is to make everybody in the firm—something like 600 people working in this multinational company— sensitive to the environment, aware of environmental hazards, and trained in environmental safety and conservation.

He seemed to be doing a very good job, as indicated by his very quick promotion in the company. However this son always leaves his lights and his air conditioner on when he leaves the house in the morning. He cannot observe minimum conservation rules in his own behavior. Here is a person who is very compassionate, passionate, and well-educated, who is helping others in environmental affairs, but yet his own behavior in the house does not resemble what he is training people to be.

This brings us to the matter of education. How could a person be so transformed on the cognitive level, but yet on the behavioral level not be able to turn off his lights and the air conditioner when he leaves? My son's mother and I have even argued with him about this several times and he promises that he will change. By the way, Egypt is a hot country; we use air conditioning for about eight months of the year.

In short, despite all of our efforts, my son's mother and I have failed to change this one item of his behavior. This case tells us a great deal about what lies ahead in terms of what to do.

We have these tons of knowledge. The quality and the quantity of it are overwhelming. The questions are how to convert this knowledge into programs of action, and how to change people's behavior. It is an immense challenge.

I would like to share several thoughts regarding this task, even though I should not claim authoritative knowledge on this, since I failed with my own son. As is true with all teachers, even though we fail, we keep preaching.

Including the Great Communicators

My first message has to do with what I would call "the missing people," people who cannot only take this knowledge that we have in abundance and convert it into do-able programs and modules for action but who also can communicate. The great communicators.

This is really one constituency, one stakeholder, that we are missing in this session and in this conference: the great communicator. I have listed who the great communicators are today.

We have, for example, the educators, the teachers; many of us have taught in one form or another as academics. The challenge is not just with our own university students: It is with the hundreds of millions of pre-college students around the world.

Teachers are an important constituency that has to be incorporated into an environmental movement, with the knowledge that we have been accumulating here this week—in the last 20 years in fact. Through the teachers, knowledge could be both simplified and turned into educational models.

The second constituency that I feel must be present somehow is the mass communicators themselves, the people who are working in the media—in the press, radio, and television. These media of mass communication have proven to be even more effective than schooling in terms of changing people's perceptions and attitudes, and possibly people's behavior.

The third constituency that is missing from this occasion is the preachers. We heard on two or three occasions when we were listening at the ethics and values workshop this week that preachers still have a tremendous weight with ordinary people everywhere. These important sharers of words and thoughts have to be somehow incorporated into our movement for converting knowledge into action.

The fourth constituency is entertainers and sports people. If they can be converted to our message, they could become role models far more influential than anyone can imagine, more than the most eloquent lecturers and scientists.

These are, therefore, the four constituencies that I feel must be incorporated into our effort and given a clear, simple message.

The last point that I would like to emphasize in this presentation is that the earlier we start with children, the more effective we can be in terms of behavioral change. One reason for my failure with my son is that I started relatively late. He was already 20 years old and his behavior was already shaped.

Two Powerful Examples

In terms of the possibilities of behavioral change, we were recently reminded how people living even in the most primitive and simple of surroundings can tune in to the communicators. The events that brought home powerfully how people can be touched were the deaths of Lady Diana and Mother Teresa.

Different as these two human beings were, they both seemed to have captured the imagination of people across class lines, generations, and cultures.

We ask the question, "Why?" For Diana, perhaps, it was her glamour and her royalty. And for Mother Teresa? She was almost the opposite of Diana in terms of appearance, height, and seeking glamour. Yet both of these persons captured the imagination of everyone, including people in my country.

What lessons from these two people who were great communicators are here for us in putting forward an idea—sustainable development—that we know needs to reach the hearts and minds of people and to bring about change?

A Surprising Human Response

Let me elaborate my point with a story. It has to do with a British journalist who happened to be in my country when Diana died. He is a senior correspondent of *The Guardian*. He had been in the country on a different assignment altogether, but when Diana and her boyfriend, an Egyptian, died a tragic death, he was asked by his newspaper to find out the reactions of Egyptians.

He called me and he said, "You know, I've been given this assignment, I'd like to know your reaction to the event." I said, "Well, my reaction is one of shock, of grief." He said, "What about the Egyptian people?" I said, "I do not know about the Egyptian people. You are calling me at 9:00 o'clock in the morning and I can only give you my reaction and my family's reaction."

I told him that if he was interested in knowing the reaction of the Egyptian people, I was going to a community in the afternoon, a shantytown that is one of the worst slum areas of Cairo, and he was welcome to accompany me if he wished. The man, whose Arabic is very good, jumped at the opportunity. He came with me and we started going through the slum.

The area is one square kilometer, yet half a million people live in it. Until recently, those people did not have a school, a hospital, or even a police station. It was a suffering human jungle. The government discovered the negligence of the area three or four years ago and started to do a few things. The reason I go there regularly is to check on the government programs that are trying to upgrade services there.

To his amazement, the British journalist found that everybody in that slum area knew about the death of Diana, knew about her boyfriend and all the details.

This was four o'clock in the afternoon. The accident had taken place seven or eight hours earlier, but to the journalist's amazement, not only did the people know all the details of the accident, they knew a lot about the life of Princess Diana. He wrote and filed his story. The only part that he could not readily comprehend is that people did not think it was an accident: they thought there must be a conspiracy behind it.

When we went back to the area a week later, we found the same interest and level of detailed knowledge. Where had people gotten their information? They basically got it from the media, especially from television. For people anywhere in the world who might be under the poverty line and may be downtrodden, television has become a standard item in their homes.

When the British journalist came with me the second time, we tried to learn what the people saw in common between Princess Diana and Mother Teresa. One of the key items was emphasized by a commentor in this meeting: passion. Princess Diana and Mother Teresa were passionate about certain things, and that had carried through to everybody, even people who did not know the details of what Princess Diana and Mother Teresa had been doing in their lives.

Need for a Passionate Message

Concern, compassion, passion, and sincerity; once you have these elements people listen, the message gets across. That may be an important lesson for all of us in our effort to convert this qualitatively superb and huge quantity of knowledge about sustainable development into something that people cannot only respond to, but also act on. People are willing to act if the message gets to them clearly, and if they know that the messenger is sincere.

How to Proceed—How to Connect?

Clovis Maksoud

When we talk about organizing knowledge, we should next reflect on the question "organizing it for what?" We certainly need to ask how knowledge can be organized when we are living in a situation that is disorganized globally and at times in specific areas of the world.

As we consider the matter of organizing knowledge at this juncture, the context is that we are faced with a world in which two simultaneous yet conflicting trends are taking place. On the one hand there is the globalization of issues—environment and human rights—and on the other there is the fragmentation of civil and political societies and states in many developing areas.

How can we help these failed societies and fragmented countries so that they can organize their own knowledge about global issues? This question might appear to be paradoxical, but it reflects the challenge of a new reality in which governments have to reconcile fragmentation with globalization.

Understanding Differences around the World

To be of assistance, we have to sort out the various priorities around the world. Often the priority in developing countries—the Global South—is that in front of the quest for quality of life, which in the final analysis is the outcome of genuine knowledge, comes the matter of survival. In the North, with a few individual exceptions, the search for quality of life is the object. Thus, having survival as the priority means that there is bound to be a difference between the South and the North in values and moral attitudes.

In a globalized economy and in the globalization of issues that we face there is the question of the future for pluralistic societies. Further, in terms of acquiring and sustaining knowledge, we see that in many parts of the world the state subsumes society, instead of society and the state being in partnership. Interesting as well is the evidence against the prevailing notion that democratization and a free market inevitably go together. We have seen how in a number of instances the free market has been transformed into something that I would call the "loose" market. In some areas of the North, and especially in the East in the former Soviet Union, free market conditions that might serve as a possible precedent for democratization have led not only to a great deal of corruption, but to something quite different from a healthy free market.

By the same token we have seen economic elites in some developing countries linking up with a global constituency and tearing themselves away from social involvement in the rebuilding of their own societies and states. Many such examples could be cited.

Nature of Modern Knowledge

I would also like to make this observation: Knowledge is a peculiar process. It should involve continuous learning, but it also necessitates some unlearning of things that we thought we had known. It is in this process of both learning and unlearning that we have sometimes been deficient. As a result some of the things that we have learned in the past become dead weight on our capacity to learn anew and move ahead.

There is another point I would like to make about learning and knowledge: In this period we are witnessing what I called earlier the CNN-ization of information. Of course this means we are instantly informed. We know what is taking place within an hour of a revolt somewhere, or progress somewhere. Our ability to transform this information into knowledge is deficient, because the component of factual analysis that we are presented with is lacking.

Of course there are the news commentators. Their opinions often are informed, but these observers tend to substitute for the long-range process of professors, intellectuals, and philosophers who could offer a greater depth of knowledge and understanding of today's world.

This is an important development, because when I feel that I am instantly cognizant of events, with the aid of the commentators, I tend to be satisfied without the pursuit of further analysis, and thus I, and I am sure many others, become satisfied with half-truths.

The job of organizing knowledge must always take place in the context of these realities, taking account of and dealing with them. In a way, also, we see a segmented, fragmented approach to sustainable development, just as in the contemporary characteristics of knowledge, but I note that there are many who want to bring about an integrated approach to sustainability.

The Global South and Sustainable Development

One of the speakers today mentioned that there is a need for central authority, but that it also should include the delegation and devolution of power. This approach must be built into our organizational and institutional infrastructures. Otherwise, authority will simply be dispersed.

The point should be made, however, that in order for authority to be able to effectively delegate power, it must be realized that, especially in the Global South, what is legal is not always legitimate, and what is legitimate is not always legal. My point is that as we study the questions of legality and legitimacy in countries, we find that sometimes, where they ought to be coterminous they are divided. These realities might exist in more diluted versions in the West, but they certainly are a stark reality in many parts of the Global South.

What brings this to the forefront of our consciousness is the fact that it is going to be necessary to extend our moral compass across time, among generations, across space, among nations, and within nations, concerning ourselves with many complex issues and concerns across the range of humanity.

Let me mention a principle that applies to the sustainable development doctrine. It is the precautionary principle, a part of international law. It is another version of what is being marketed today as preventive diplomacy.

Importantly, preventive action should not only be taught as part of knowledge, but knowledge really needs to come with what is called structural prevention, which is, in the final analysis, equivalent to development in a comprehensive, holistic sense.

In the academic field, to convey their interdisciplinary, holistic character, issues of the Global South and of sustainable development should be crosslisted in most, if not all, of the constituent colleges of universities. This is important because it would bring together issues of gender, population, environmental quality, and human rights as a part of development studies, as well as other aspects of education and knowledge.

I will note here, by the way, that human rights is one of the major challenges of our time. Nevertheless, we must realize that the issue is not confined to notions of freedom of speech and assembly or access to an independent judiciary, vital and important and ennobling as these rights are.

Instead, human *needs* must become an integral, organic part of the idea of human rights. This inclusiveness of human needs into the human rights concept, especially in the Global South, must be achieved in a very convincing manner, not as a patronizing dispensation.

Public's View of Sovereignty

I would make another comment related to human rights. In a way that was hinted at this morning, sovereignty can be a pretext for dictatorial regimes and authoritarian governments to disallow any kind of universal or regional concerns in the persistent violation of human rights.

However, I would caution us not to dismiss sovereignty as merely a block preventing humanitarian or human rights intervention. Sovereignty for many countries in the Global South is a very cherished legacy. It has resulted from the struggles for independence of these countries, struggles producing martyrs and national heroes.

Thus in the organization of our knowledge, it is important not to mix up the meanings of sovereignty in the Global South. The international community needs to be able to discern the difference between the assertion of sovereignty as a cherished legacy and as a pretext for suppression and obfuscation.

I will refer now to another major issue that we are witnessing, and being a new professor myself, I am experiencing it firsthand. The issue has to do with the dialogue among generations, as characterized by our terms of reference, our narrative, the words we use. In fact there has been a dialogue *at* the younger generation rather than a dialogue *with* it. Working properly, the learning and unlearning process I referred to earlier takes place as the younger people learn from us, as teachers, and as we learn from them by unlearning some of the patterns that we have developed.

Education and Truth

Now let me respond to Professor Saad Eddin's comments about the role of preachers as communicators. I am of two minds about it. Not all preachers communicate viable options; that leaves us with the challenge of distinguishing between simplified communication and simplistic communication. Some preachers and some politicians address the complexity of our issues with oversimplified answers. That, in my view, is a prescription for suppression and demagoguery.

Certainly, simplifying answers is a task of knowledge; it is one important communication dimension. In contrast, though, the simplistic answer can be an advertisement of half-truths in order to give legitimacy to bad intentions, such as authoritarian regimes.

In comparison to going down the wrong path to simplistic answers, I would say that education is an enabling process for what is important. It is important that our access to new knowledge be continuous, just as the development of the new knowledge is continuous. In this way knowledge can become a tool to at least approximate truth.

In the final analysis as we live from one generation to the other, there are so many truths. The task of what might be called "sustainably relevant knowledge" is to bring these truths together so that they can reinforce each other in coherent policies and behavior.

My last point is that there are key global constituencies in the NGO communities. There are the families, environmentalists, human rights activists, and people who are interested in urbanization problems.

In a way these constituencies have a hyphenated identity: I am an Egyptian environmentalist. I am an Egyptian feminist. I am part of an Egyptian family. The situation applies among NGOs all over the world.

In fact NGOs can be very useful. Unfortunately, though, they do not coordinate to provide the dynamism or vitality or a coherent sense of direction. Feminists might say, "Well, our interest is not in improving the environment." Human rights activists might say, "Feminist issues are not something that we have to deal with."

It is important that these organs of civil society come together so that they can make their impact felt and channel their energies. If they manage to do so, they would resolve not only the crisis of identity in their global citizenship but would also be helping to bring society and the state into partnership. This is where the universities and knowledge come in.

Appendix A
Program

Organizing Knowledge for Environmentally Sustainable Development

A Concurrent Meeting of the Fifth Annual World Bank Conference
on Environmentally and Socially Sustainable Development
Cosponsored by UNESCO and the World Bank
Held at the World Bank, Washington, D.C.
October 9–10, 1997

Setting the Agenda
> *Tariq Husain*, Director, Learning and Leadership Center, World Bank
> *Benjamin Ladner*, President, American University
> *Gustavo López Ospina*, Director, Transdisciplinary Project on Educating for a Sustainable
> Future, UNESCO

Shifting Gears for the Application of Knowledge
> *Don Aitkin*, Vice Chancellor and President, University of Canberra

Shifting Requirements for Knowledge to Advance a Sustainable South
> *Partha Dasgupta*, Professor of Economics, Cambridge University
Discussion

What Are the Obligations of Academic Leaders to the Demands of Sustainable Development?
Moderator: *Wadi Haddad*, Special Advisor to the Director General, UNESCO
Panelists: *Alvaro Umana*, Professor and Director of the Natural Resources Management Program,
> INCAE
> *Veena Das*, Professor of Sociology, Delhi University

**The Critical Path: Linking Knowledge to Advance Environmentally and Socially Sustainable
Development**
> *Kenneth Prewitt*, President, Social Science Research Council, on behalf of the Task Force
> on Higher Education in Society

The Social–Natural Science Gap in Educating for Sustainable Development
> *Ismail Serageldin*, Vice President, Environmentally and Socially Sustainable
> Development, World Bank
> *Peter Thatcher*, Environmental Advisor and Specialist

Global Ecosystem Governance and Transboundary Requirements
> *Claudio Grossman*, Dean, Washington College of Law, American University
Discussion

Knowledge, Finance, and Sustainable Development
>   *Vinod Thomas*, Director, Economic Development Institute, World Bank
>   *Theodore Panayotou*, HIID, Harvard University

Discussion

How to Proceed—How to Connect?
>   *Saad Eddin Ibrahim*, Chairman, Ibn Kahldoun Center for Development Studies
>   *Clovis Maksoud*, Director, Center for the Global South, American University

Appendix B
Presenters

Don Aitkin
Vice Chancellor and President
University of Canberra
PO Box 1 Belconen ACT 2616, Australia
Tel: (61-606) 201-5000
Fax: (61-606) 201-5036

Veena Das
Head, Department of Sociology
Delhi University
India
Fax: (9111) 7257858

Partha Dasgupta
Professor of Economics
University of Cambridge
Sidgwick Avenue
Cambridge CB3 9DD, UK
Tel: (44-1223) 335-206
Fax: (44-1223) 335-475

Claudio Grossman
Dean
Washington College of Law
American University
4801 Massachusetts Avenue, NW
Washington, DC 20016-8192, USA
Tel: (202) 274-4002
Fax: (202) 274-4005

Wadi Haddad
Special Advisor to the Director General
UNESCO
7 place de Fontenoy 75352
Paris 07 SP, France

Benjamin Ladner
President
American University
4400 Massachusetts Avenue, NW
Washington, DC 20016-8061, USA
Tel: (202) 885-2121
Fax: (202) 885-3265

Clovis Maksoud
Director
Center for the Global South
American University
Washington, DC, USA
Tel: (202) 885-1612
Fax (202) 885-1186

Gustavo López Ospina
Director
Transdisciplinary Project on Educating
for a Sustainable Future (EPD)
UNESCO
7 place de Fontenoy 75352
Paris 07 SP, France
Tel: (33-14) 568-0569/0868
Fax: (33-14) 568-5635

Theodore Panayotou
Professor
Harvard Institute for International
    Development
Harvard University
One Elliot Street
Cambridge, MA 02138, USA
Tel: (617) 495-9173
Fax: (617) 496-3956
E-mail: tpanayot@hiid.harvard.edu

Kenneth Prewitt
President
Social Science Research Council
810 Seventh Avenue
New York, NY 10019, USA
Tel: (212) 377-2700
Fax: (212) 377-2727
E-mail: prewitt@ssrc.org

Peter Thacher
Environmental Specialist and Advisor
54 Gold Street
Stonington, CT 06378-1229, US
Tel: (203) 535-0633
Fax: (203 535-4787
E-mail: pthacher@igc.apc.org

Alvo Umana
Professor and Director
Natural Resources Management Program
    (INCAE)
La Garita, Alajuela, Costa Rica
Tel: (506) 260-4162
Fax: (506) 443-0506

Jerzy A. Wojciechowski
Professor of Philosophy Emeritus
University of Ottawa
Canada

World Bank Group Staff
All staff can be reached at 1818 H Street, NW
Washington, DC 20433, USA

Tariq Husain
Senior Advisor
Capacity Building
Operational Core Services
Room MC10-377
Tel: (202) 473-3907
Fax: (202) 522-0365

Ismail Serageldin
Vice President
Special Programs
Room MC4-123
Tel: (202) 473-4502
Fax: (202) 473-3112

Vinod Thomas
Director
Economic Development Institute
Room G5-003
Tel: (202) 473-6300
Fax: (202) 522-1714

Appendix C
Report of the UNESCO Secretary General to the Commission on Sustainable Development
(Sixth Session, 20 April to 1 May 1998)
Chapter 36 of Agenda 21: Education,
Public Awareness, and Training
(Excerpt from document E/CN.17/1998/5)

A. Current Status and Trends

15. The first report on education, public awareness and training was submitted by UNESCO to the CSD at its fourth session in 1996. At that time, a special work programme was initiated in which priorities for action and key actors were designated. The nineteenth special session of the UN General Assembly gave added impetus to Chapter 36 implementation. The information provided below includes an expanded version of the work programme initiated in 1996. Additional information on the issues addressed here can be found in E/CN.17/1998/5/Add.2.

16. There is growing recognition within political and economic circles of the critical role of education as part of the enabling framework for sustainable development. Education is now widely acknowledged as a means to prepare people to engage with governments, business and industry; to support changes in governance and the marketplace; and to adapt to a complex and rapidly changing world. Ministries of finance and planning, as well as other sectoral ministries, are increasingly targeting education as an underpinning for solving economic, social and political problems. Education is recognized as a driving force for changing values and mind sets, which can in turn lead to behavioural change. Education is an integral element in debates on such key issues as poverty, population, health, employment, environmental management, consumption and production and technology transfer, all of which are essential ingredients of sustainable development.

17. It is increasingly recognized that sustainable development encompasses all disciplines, and requires that education acknowledge the disciplines in their relationship to each other, engaging all levels and forms. Education does not mean formal education alone. It includes non-formal and informal modes of teaching and learning, such as those that take place in the home and community.

18. The background document entitled "Educating for a sustainable future: a transdis-ciplinary vision for concerted action," is meant to provide a conceptual framework and serve as the basis for regional strategy papers, or action programmes. The intersessional conference of experts on "Environment and Society: Education and Public Awareness for Sustainability" co-organized by UNESCO and the Government of Greece in

Thessaloniki in 1997, addressed this issue, as did numerous other meetings held during 1997 to celebrate the twentieth anniversary of the Tbilisi conference on environmental education, including the Conference PlanetERE held in Montreal in 1997 for Francophone countries.

19. To accelerate progress towards sustainable development, emphasis has been shifting to action at national and local levels. An important theme continues to be inadequate financing for education, despite the consensus among governments of its importance. This evolution has important implications for how institutions orient their work and for the allocation of resources. The UN system, for example, is working to improve coordination of services at country level. To support this, UNESCO is launching an inter-agency initiative on educating for a sustainable future in a number of countries.

20. The creativity and risk-taking required for innovation in educational institutions, in meeting new challenges, are diminished by downsizing, reductions in resources, and heightened competition. Moreover, experience has shown that partnerships "in the abstract" tend to divert energy and resources without delivering concrete results. The increasing emphasis on work at country level is expected to help focus joint efforts, since alliances and partnerships tend to be most effective when they are centred on concrete initiatives where the contribution of each partner is essential to achieving common and concrete goals.

B. Action Required

21. Further to the programme of work on education and public awareness adopted in 1996, the following sub-programmes and partnerships in implementation are presented below for further consideration. Once agreed, progress made in implementing the work programme should be monitored on a regular basis.

(1) *Clarifying the Concept and Key Messages of Education for Sustainable Development*

22. The concept and key messages must be further developed and implanted at regional and national levels, by: (i) preparing regional education strategy papers which would in turn be taken up at the national level; (ii) analysing the action plans of all the major UN conferences, the conventions on biological diversity, climate change and desertification, the UN Agenda for Development, and regional action plans for sustain-ability, with a view to promoting the integrated follow-up to these agreements with respect to education and public awareness under the umbrella of chapter 36; (iii) formulating the core messages of education for sustainable development which need to be communicated at all levels of education and through all channels, and mobilizing diverse networks of experts to this end.

23. Governments and the media are encouraged to undertake information campaigns to communicate to the public the key messages of sustainable development. Governments should provide incentives to the media for this purpose.

(2) *Reviewing National Education Policies and Reorienting Formal Educational Systems*

24. Governments are urged to develop, within five years, policy statements for reorienting education towards sustainable development, including a definition of what needs to be done at local, national and regional levels, so that all actors will understand their respective roles and responsibilities. The participation of local authorities and other local actors in this process should be ensured. The UN system, other governmental and non-governmental organizations, and the education and scientific communities are called on to provide assistance to this endeavour.

25. Priority needs to be given to teacher training in reorienting formal education systems. The approximately 60 million teachers worldwide need to be engaged in this process. Governments are urged to ensure that within five years measures have been taken in this direction. International and national representatives of teachers (including unions) should be involved, as well as specialists in higher education.

26. Institutions of higher education should adapt their teaching and research to promoting an in-

terdisciplinary approach conducive to addressing sustainable development issues. Governments and the academic community are urged to support this process. The World Conference on Higher Education in 1998, and its follow-up, should give due consideration to the reform of higher education systems to support sustainable development. Likewise, the World Science Conference in 1999 should consider how to ensure that educational reform draws on scientific knowledge and how to integrate knowledge emanating from the disciplines in the service of sustainable development.

27. In view of the long-term implications of educational reform, Governments need to ensure the continuity needed for reform efforts to be fully implemented. Progress made in this regard should be regularly monitored at the international level.

(3) *Incorporating Education into National Strategies and Action Plans for Sustainable Development*

28. Education and public awareness should be made significant components in regional, national and local strategies and plans for sustainable development. Governments, working with civil society, the private sector, the education community and others need to ensure such integration. National and local governments are encouraged to establish national and local committees for this purpose, which should be interdisciplinary, involve all sectors, and ensure full participation of both governmental and non-governmental bodies. The United Nations system, in partnerships with other key international institutions, should be called upon to assist in the integration of educational concerns into such strategies and plans at country level. A survey of existing regional and national strategies and plans to determine the extent to which education has been adequately addressed, initiated by UNESCO, in cooperation with DESA and UNDP, should be completed and recommendations developed on that basis.

(4) *Educating to Promote Sustainable Consumption and Production Patterns*

29. Initiatives are needed to link the work programmes on education and on changing consumption and production patterns. Such initiatives could include raising awareness of the implications of current unsustainable patterns of consumption and production; dissemination of the revised guidelines for consumer protection; partnerships with industries and the media to work out strategies for advertising; making use of educational tools and consumer feedback mechanisms to facilitate policy-making; and developing and promoting social instruments through education and training intended to change consumption and production patterns. The task managers for chapters 4 and 36 (UN-DESA and UNESCO), working together with other relevant organizations, including UNEP, the OECD and representatives of business and industry, should develop concrete recommendations for initiatives along these lines.

(5) *Analysing and Redirecting Investments in Education*

30. The proposed review by the international financial institutions on current investment in education from the perspective of sustainable development, should also consider financing by Governments and by major groups. Based on such a review, a strategy for mobilizing greater resources to finance education from all sources should be developed.

(6) *Identifying and Sharing Innovative Practices*

31. It is important to continue to identify and share innovative practices in support of education and public awareness for sustainability, at local, national, regional and international levels. An international electronic registry is being developed by UNESCO, with the assistance of the Government of the United States, to address this need by establishing a second generation web site and a knowledge management system for chapter Innovative case studies from non-conventional sources, such as various major groups including industries, women, youth and NGOs, should be included in such an inventory. Regional networks and fora for sharing innovative practices should be encouraged.

(7) Partnerships in Implementation

32. The following are some ways in which partnerships can be further strengthened.

(i)   Public-private cooperation should continue to be enhanced for launching effective education and training of workers, as well as undertaking public awareness campaigns, including through media and advertisement, in promoting sustainable consumption and production patterns, use of environmentally sound technologies and in communicating other key issues of sustainable development.

(ii) The involvement of the scientific and technological community in enriching education, training and awareness-raising programmes needs to be enhanced, particularly to promote the understanding of crucial sustainable development issues of concern at local and national levels.

(iii) Youth have been important advocates for sustainable development, especially at the community level. Innovative programmes such as the Youth indicators programme should be identified, encouraged and new ones developed. At the same time, they should be made part of national dialogues and decision-making on education.

(iv) Women, especially in rural communities, usually play a key role in the economic as well as in the social and cultural aspects of life. The local community and the household are important entry points for messages on sustainable development, especially for adults and out-of-school children. Programmes to strengthen the role of women in these contexts should be promoted.

(v)   Non-governmental organizations are critical partners in catalysing action and awareness raising for advancing sustainable development and mobilizing civil society to take initiatives in their communities. The role of NGOs at the national and local levels is growing exponentially and their innovative practices should be widely disseminated.

Appendix D
The Ecology of Knowledge

Jerzy Wojciechowski

There is an essential difference between past and present problems of humanity. In the earlier epochs there was little effective knowledge, and human beings faced the greatest challenge not from other humans, threatening as they were, but from nature. Nature was life-giving but overwhelming. People could fight other people, but they could only fear and worship nature. The present generation neither fears nor venerates nature. Unbelievable as it may sound, all the great problems of the present times are direct or indirect efforts of the development of rational knowledge of its systematic application to the satisfaction of human desires, as desires are fanned by growing knowledge and the resulting ability to do things.

The positive feedback existing between knowledge and desires is the direct cause of our present predicament. Such problems as overpopulation, pollution, growing inequalities among nations and cultures, atomic weapons, and future shock are not of nature's making. They are knowledge-based, human problems. What is more, they are the products of Western rationality. We cannot blame them on accidental developments, on fate, or on occult forces beyond our reckoning. All these problems are the logical outcome of a long-lasting, constantly growing, systematic effort of the brightest minds pursuing the Western ideal of rational knowledge. The irony of the situation is that the dimension of these problems is the proof of the scope of the intellectual achievements that make them possible.

This again is not accidental. Let us express the relationship between problems and knowledge in the following way:

Law I. The Size and the Complexity of Knowledge-Generated Problems is Proportional to the Level of Knowledge.

Whoever reflects on the situation of humanity cannot but be struck by the role that Western culture has played in bringing it about. All cultures develop a system of knowledge, but Western cultures have developed the most powerful type of knowledge, science, and technology to a higher degree than anyone else. Moreover, the West has always viewed knowledge as the most perfect human product and valued in mind as the highest human faculty. It is therefore not surprising that it considers the continuous development of knowledge as a major personal and social goal. Admirable as this attitude may be, it does raise some difficult questions.

We would have to be very uncritical to imagine that the way Western people think is the best way possible, that their hierarchy of values is fully satisfactory for solving present problems of humanity and for guiding it into a more adequate, sustainable future mode of existence. Obviously, this is not the case. As stated by Law I, our knowledge generates problems as much as it solves them. The hierarchy of values that has fuelled the development of Western culture is largely responsible for the situation we are in.

Editor's note: This paper is included as relevant to the conference discussions.

It would be rather naïve to believe that it does not require some improvement.

Culture-bashing may be politically correct, but we must realize that our culture has failed for the same reason that it has been so successful. It has developed a powerful type of knowledge, and has used it efficiently to satisfy human desires.

The demiurgic powers unleashed by the development of Western rationality have been, until recently, our pride and joy. Now they are viewed with increasing concern. This concern has not been addressed by the philosophers who have been concerned with questions of the nature of knowledge, problems of truth, and the objectivity or logical structure of thinking. Nevertheless, they always viewed knowledge as an eminently positive fact, the most perfect achievement of the rational animal. They never looked at the body of knowledge as an entity distinct from knowers. Consequently, they never studied the relationship existing between knowers and the body of knowledge (the knowledge construct—KC), and did not ask whether this relationship is always positive or whether it may also be at times negative. In light of the present predicament, this question has to be asked. It means that the relationship of the knower to the KC has to be considered in a more critical manner than it has been until now. Perhaps this way we will be able to better understand why the development of knowledge is a source of problems.

Knowledge is the product of the act of knowing. It would seem therefore that knowledge should be more knowable than anything else. This, however, is not the case. Knowledge is obscure and difficult to know, and so are its consequences. Contrary to what Plato and his school believed, every act of knowledge produces immediate or more distant effects of a diverse nature, both in the subjective and objective world. Some of these effects are intentional, others are not; some are foreseeable, many are not; some are good, others are bad. The important fact is that the sum total of the consequences of an act of knowledge is not a finite set that can be circumscribed and determined in advance. The predicament in which humanity finds itself presently is the best illustration of this situation.

Our present predicament is not a fortuitous event. It occurs at the time of the most advanced state of knowledge in human history. In order to understand the condition of humanity and its causes, it is essential to realize the role that knowledge and its development plays in producing this situation. This is why we are forced to think about knowledge, whether or not we are interested in philosophical problems. It seems like a strange paradox, but the more knowledge advances, the more we have to worry about it. The more knowledge is powerful, the more we have to be concerned with it and with its impact on us and on the outside world. The more knowledge there is, the more problematic it is for us, and the more urgent becomes the problem. Let us express this relationship in the form of the following laws:

Law II. The Problem of Knowledge Is Proportional to the Level of Knowledge.

Law III. The Urgency of Understanding the Causality of Knowledge Is Proportional to the Level of Knowledge.

These laws go against the traditional perception of knowledge in Western culture. It is especially baffling for those who make knowing their profession. But the question of the role of knowledge in causing our present predicament cannot be simply dismissed or overlooked. The impact of knowledge is too powerful for that; its consequences too important. Moreover, if we want to understand why the development of knowledge creates a growing moral problem, we will have to look into this question.

Humans as Demiurgos

Science and technology have succeeded and failed at the same time. Our evaluation of these two modes of knowledge depends on how we look at them. Seen in themselves, they are spectacularly successful both in their present accomplishments and in the vistas that they open up for their further development. Through science and technology we know more and more about nature and gain increasingly greater dominion over it. In the process we make possible the expansion of the human biomass. However when we look at science and technology in a larger context, we get a very different picture.

It is the other side of the coin that makes us pause and question the value of our scientific achievements.

Because of the success of science and technology, until recently it looked as if we had found the magic formula for an earthly paradise. If the mirage of an earthly paradise is now dissipating before our eyes, it is not because we have stopped developing knowledge; it is not because of science and technology as such that we are beginning to question their value. *What has changed is our perception of the broader contact in and from which these modes of knowledge are seen and judged.* The context in question is the relationship of humans to nature.

Either humans are seen as part of nature or as standing above nature. It is worth reminding ourselves that neither of these views was formed in a scientific manner. Both are much older than science. The second way of conceiving the human–nature relationship is much more unusual. Indeed, it is unique in the world. It is exclusive to Western culture and it has produced and continues to produce extraordinary consequences. As far as we can tell, its source, or at least its first written expression, is the famous sentence in the Book of Genesis. What the Hebraic religion did was to assign to humans a special position above all other creatures and authorize them to rule over nature. This idea, taken up by Christianity, became the cornerstone of modern Western culture. The ideas of Francis Bacon and the ideology of progress are the direct descendants of this religious conviction. It is in a sense ironic that a religious idea has helped to shape the worldview of the modern, increasingly nonreligious, culture. This is a perfect illustration of the fact, stated earlier, that the sum total of the consequences of intellectual constructs cannot be foreseen or determined in advance.

As we said above, neither of the two ways of seeing the relationship between humans and nature is scientific; this is not only because these views are older than science. There is another, more formal reason for that. Both views imply value judgments—that one way of looking at nature is better than another. Science instead is supposed to be an objective, value-free cognition based on observation and formulating verifiable propositions. Science can and does tell us what

kind of impact on nature a particular human activity has, but science cannot tell us what the place of humans is in nature. To answer this question we would have to know not only why there are humans on Earth but also why humans are as they are, that is, why do they have the nature they have? To be more precise, why do they have an intellect capable of producing knowledge that no other animal can produce? Why does the desire for knowledge transcend the physical needs of the human body?

Even if science cannot answer these specific questions, it does not mean that no progress can be made in trying to elucidate the human-nature relationship. It is through scientific research that we gain a better understanding of the consequences of human activity, and it is science that makes us aware of the fact that we cannot continue to behave as we do. The crucial point in this respect is the realization that nature is not inexhaustible. If the Earth system to which we are bound were inexhaustible, it would not matter much what we do to it. The ecological problem would be nonexistent, and there would be no significant difference betweeen the consequences of the belief that humans are part of nature and the other belief that places them above nature. Consequently the development of knowledge would not pose a moral problem.

Unfortunately, this is not the case. The finiteness of the Earth system does not allow an indefinite expansion of human physical activity. At a certain point the feedback existing between human activity and its consequences changes from positive to negative. In other words the pursuit of satisfaction of our needs and desires turns sour. The situation we are in, because of our demiurgic powers, forces us to be increasingly more aware of our condition and of the consequences of our behavior, whether we like it or not. The more we know, the more evident is this unpleasant necessity. This is by now public knowledge. The question that remains wide open is the meaning of the present situation. Does our predicament have a redeeming value? Is it an evolutionary device forcing us to evolve to a higher stage of intellectual and moral development, or does it portend doom? One thing is certain: The demiurgic power that we have developed with the aid of our knowledge will not allow humanity to remain in the present state for long.

Moral Problematic

Morals are the field of value judgments. The consequences of knowledge are subject to moral judgments and always have been. What is new is the realization of the ambivalence of their value. The reason for the change in our appreciation of the worth of knowledge and its consequences is the same as the reason for the change in the perception of our activity in general— namely, the realization of the finiteness of natural resources. Basically, it is a question of proportionality existing between humans and natural environment.

As we know from mathematics, there is no definite relationship between a number, no matter how big, and infinity; but there is a relationship between two finite numbers. In the latter case, the proportionality can be calculated. With the development of the science of ecology and the preoccupation with a sustainable mode of life, we began to calculate the proportionality existing between us and the nature we depend on for survival. This calculation may easily turn out to be the most important mathematical operation ever undertaken.

Ethics involves responsibility. We are responsible for what we do consciously and with adequate knowledge. Moral responsibility is nothing new, but the context of responsibility has changed dramatically. The Judeo-Christian system of ethics is based on the Ten Commandments. The problem is that the Ten Commandments no longer encompass the variety of human activities. If Moses went up Mount Sinai today, he would come back not with ten but with many more commandments.

The development of knowledge renders the existing ethical systems more and more inadequate. At the same time, it makes ethical judgments more and more necessary. Let us express the relationship between knowledge and its development on the one hand, and the need of ethical considerations on the other, in the following way:

Law IV. The Need for Ethical Evaluation of Knowledge and of Its Consequences Is Proportional to the Power of Knowledge.

Law V. The Adequacy of Traditional Ethical Systems Is Inversely Proportional to the Power of Knowledge.

The need to improve the existing systems of ethics may well be the most valuable consequence of the development of knowledge and the most unexpected as well. It is not unreasonable to imply that the impact of the development of knowledge on ethics is, or at least indicates, the metaphysical reason of this development. Furthermore, it may point to the ultimate character of the evolution of humanity.

Distributors of World Bank Publications

Prices and credit terms vary from country to country. Consult your local distributor before placing an order.

ARGENTINA
Oficina del Libro Internacional
Av. Cordoba 1877
1120 Buenos Aires
Tel: (54 11) 815-8354
Fax: (54 11) 815-8156
E-mail: olilibro@satlink.com

AUSTRALIA, FIJI, PAPUA NEW GUINEA, SOLOMON ISLANDS, VANUATU, AND SAMOA
D.A. Information Services
648 Whitehorse Road
Mitcham 3132
Victoria
Tel: (61) 3 9210 7777
Fax: (61) 3 9210 7788
E-mail: service@dadirect.com.au

AUSTRIA
Gerold and Co.
Weihburggasse 26
A-1011 Wien
Tel: (43 1) 512-47-31-0
Fax: (43 1) 512-47-31-29

BANGLADESH
Micro Industries Development
Assistance Society (MIDAS)
House 5, Road 16
Dhanmondi R/Area
Dhaka 1209
Tel: (880 2) 326427
Fax: (880 2) 811188

BELGIUM
Jean De Lannoy
Av. du Roi 202
1060 Brussels
Tel: (32 2) 538-5169
Fax: (32 2) 538-0841

BRAZIL
Publicações Tecnicas Internacionais Ltda.
Rua Peixoto Gomide, 209
01409 Sao Paulo, SP.
Tel: (55 11) 259-6644
Fax: (55 11) 258-6990
E-mail: postmaster@pti.uol.br

CANADA
Renouf Publishing Co. Ltd.
5369 Canotek Road
Ottawa, Ontario K1J 9J3
Tel: (613) 745-2665
Fax: (613) 745-7660
E-mail: order.dept@renoufbooks.com

CHINA
China Financial & Economic
Publishing House
8, Da Fo Si Dong Jie
Beijing
Tel: (86 10) 6333-8257
Fax: (86 10) 6401-7365

China Book Import Centre
P.O. Box 2825
Beijing

COLOMBIA
Infoenlace Ltda.
Carrera 6 No. 51-21
Apartado Aereo 34270
Santafé de Bogotá, D.C.
Tel: (57 1) 285-2798
Fax: (57 1) 285-2798

COTE D'IVOIRE
Center d'Edition et de Diffusion Africaines
(CEDA)
04 B.P. 541
Abidjan 04
Tel: (225) 24 6510;24 6511
Fax: (225) 25 0567

CYPRUS
Center for Applied Research
Cyprus College
6, Diogenes Street, Engomi
P.O. Box 2006
Nicosia
Tel: (357 2) 44-1730
Fax: (357 2) 46-2051

CZECH REPUBLIC
USIS, NIS Prodejna
Havelkova 22
130 00 Prague 3
Tel: (420 2) 2423 1486
Fax: (420 2) 2423 1114

DENMARK
SamfundsLitteratur
Rosenoerns Allé 11
DK-1970 Frederiksberg C
Tel: (45 31) 351942
Fax: (45 31) 357822

ECUADOR
Libri Mundi
Librería Internacional
P.O. Box 17-01-3029
Juan Leon Mera 851
Quito
Tel: (593 2) 521-606; (593 2) 544-185
Fax: (593 2) 504-209
E-mail: librimu1@librimundi.com.ec

CODEU
Ruiz de Castilla 763, Edif. Expocolor
Primer piso, Of. #2
Quito
Tel/Fax: (593 2) 507-383; 253-091
E-mail: codeu@mpsat.net.ec

EGYPT, ARAB REPUBLIC OF
Al Ahram Distribution Agency
Al Galaa Street
Cairo
Tel: (20 2) 578-6083
Fax: (20 2) 578-6833

The Middle East Observer
41, Sherif Street
Cairo
Tel: (20 2) 393-9732
Fax: (20 2) 393-9732

FINLAND
Akateeminen Kirjakauppa
P.O. Box 128
FIN-00101 Helsinki
Tel: (358 0) 121 4418
Fax: (358 0) 121-4435
E-mail: akatilaus@stockmann.fi

FRANCE
World Bank Publications
66, avenue d'Iéna
75116 Paris
Tel: (33 1) 40-69-30-56/57
Fax: (33 1) 40-69-30-68

GERMANY
UNO-Verlag
Poppelsdorfer Allee 55
53115 Bonn
Tel: (49 228) 949020
Fax: (49 228) 217492
E-mail: unoverlag@aol.com

GHANA
Epp Books Services
P.O. Box 44
TUC
Accra

GREECE
Papasotiriou S.A.
35, Stournara Str.
106 82 Athens
Tel: (30 1) 364-1826
Fax: (30 1) 364-8254

HAITI
Culture Diffusion
5, Rue Capois
C.P. 257
Port-au-Prince
Tel: (509) 23 9260
Fax: (509) 23 4858

HONG KONG, CHINA; MACAO
Asia 2000 Ltd.
Sales & Circulation Department
Seabird House, unit 1101-02
22-28 Wyndham Street, Central
Hong Kong
Tel: (852) 2530-1409
Fax: (852) 2526-1107
E-mail: sales@asia2000.com.hk

HUNGARY
Euro Info Service
Margitszigeti Europa Haz
H-1138 Budapest
Tel: (36 1) 350 80 24, 350 80 25
Fax: (36 1) 350 90 32
E-mail: euroinfo@mail.matav.hu

INDIA
Allied Publishers Ltd.
751 Mount Road
Madras - 600 002
Tel: (91 44) 852-3938
Fax: (91 44) 852-0649

INDONESIA
Pt. Indira Limited
Jalan Borobudur 20
P.O. Box 181
Jakarta 10320
Tel: (62 21) 390-4290
Fax: (62 21) 390-4289

IRAN
Ketab Sara Co. Publishers
Khaled Eslamboli Ave., 6th Street
Delafrooz Alley No. 8
P.O. Box 15745-733
Tehran 15117
Tel: (98 21) 8717819; 8716104
Fax: (98 21) 8712479
E-mail: ketab-sara@neda.net.ir

Kowkab Publishers
P.O. Box 19575-511
Tehran
Tel: (98 21) 258-3723
Fax: (98 21) 258-3723

IRELAND
Government Supplies Agency
Oifig an tSoláthair
4-5 Harcourt Road
Dublin 2
Tel: (353 1) 661-3111
Fax: (353 1) 475-2670

ISRAEL
Yozmot Literature Ltd.
P.O. Box 56055
3 Yohanan Hasandlar Street
Tel Aviv 61560
Tel: (972 3) 5285-397
Fax: (972 3) 5285-397

R.O.Y. International
PO Box 13056
Tel Aviv 61130
Tel: (972 3) 5461423
Fax: (972 3) 5461442
E-mail: royil@netvision.net.il

Palestinian Authority/Middle East
Index Information Services
P.O.B. 19502 Jerusalem
Tel: (972 2) 6271219
Fax: (972 2) 6271634

ITALY
Licosa Commissionaria Sansoni SPA
Via Duca Di Calabria, 1/1
Casella Postale 552
50125 Firenze
Tel: (55) 645-415
Fax: (55) 641-257
E-mail: licosa@ftbcc.it

JAMAICA
Ian Randle Publishers Ltd.
206 Old Hope Road, Kingston 6
Tel: 876-927-2085
Fax: 876-977-0243
E-mail: irpl@colis.com

JAPAN
Eastern Book Service
3-13 Hongo 3-chome, Bunkyo-ku
Tokyo 113
Tel: (81 3) 3818-0861
Fax: (81 3) 3818-0864
E-mail: orders@svt-ebs.co.jp

KENYA
Africa Book Service (E.A.) Ltd.
Quaran House, Mfangano Street
P.O. Box 45245
Nairobi
Tel: (254 2) 223 641
Fax: (254 2) 330 272

KOREA, REPUBLIC OF
Daejon Trading Co. Ltd.
P.O. Box 34, Youida, 706 Seoun Bldg
44-6 Youido-Dong, Yeongchengpo-Ku
Seoul
Tel: (82 2) 785-1631/4
Fax: (82 2) 784-0315

LEBANON
Librairie du Liban
P.O. Box 11-9232
Beirut
Tel: (961 9) 217 944
Fax: (961 9) 217 434

MALAYSIA
University of Malaya Cooperative
Bookshop, Limited
P.O. Box 1127
Jalan Pantai Baru
59700 Kuala Lumpur
Tel: (60 3) 756-5000
Fax: (60 3) 755-4424
E-mail: umkoop@tm.net.my

MEXICO
INFOTEC
Av. San Fernando No. 37
Col. Toriello Guerra
14050 Mexico, D.F.
Tel: (52 5) 624-2800
Fax: (52 5) 624-2822
E-mail: infotec@rtn.net.mx

Mundi-Prensa Mexico S.A. de C.V.
c/Rio Panuco, 141-Colonia Cuauhtemoc
06500 Mexico, D.F.
Tel: (52 5) 533-5658
Fax: (52 5) 514-6799

NEPAL
Everest Media International Services (P.) Ltd.
GPO Box 5443
Kathmandu
Tel: (977 1) 472 152
Fax: (977 1) 224 431

NETHERLANDS
De Lindeboom/InOr-Publikaties
P.O. Box 202, 7480 AE Haaksbergen
Tel: (31 53) 574-0004
Fax: (31 53) 572-9296
E-mail: lindeboo@worldonline.nl

NEW ZEALAND
EBSCO NZ Ltd.
Private Mail Bag 99914
New Market
Auckland
Tel: (64 9) 524-8119
Fax: (64 9) 524-8067

NIGERIA
University Press Limited
Three Crowns Building Jericho
Private Mail Bag 5095
Ibadan
Tel: (234 22) 41-1356
Fax: (234 22) 41-2056

NORWAY
NIC Info A/S
Book Department, Postboks 6512 Etterstad
N-0606 Oslo
Tel: (47 22) 97-4500
Fax: (47 22) 97-4545

PAKISTAN
Mirza Book Agency
65, Shahrah-e-Quaid-e-Azam
Lahore 54000
Tel: (92 42) 735 3601
Fax: (92 42) 576 3714

Oxford University Press
5 Bangalore Town
Sharae Faisal
PO Box 13033
Karachi-75350
Tel: (92 21) 446307
Fax: (92 21) 4547640
E-mail: ouppak@TheOffice.net

Pak Book Corporation
Aziz Chambers 21, Queen's Road
Lahore
Tel: (92 42) 636 3222; 636 0885
Fax: (92 42) 636 2328

PERU
Editorial Desarrollo SA
Apartado 3824, Lima 1
Tel: (51 14) 285380
Fax: (51 14) 286628

PHILIPPINES
International Booksource Center Inc.
1127-A Antipolo St, Barangay, Venezuela
Makati City
Tel: (63 2) 896 6501; 6505; 6507
Fax: (63 2) 896 1741

POLAND
International Publishing Service
Ul. Piekna 31/37
00-677 Warzawa
Tel: (48 2) 628-6089
Fax: (48 2) 621-7255
E-mail: books%ips@ikp.atm.com.pl

PORTUGAL
Livraria Portugal
Apartado 2681, Rua Do Carmo 70-74
1200 Lisbon
Tel: (1) 347-4982
Fax: (1) 347-0264

ROMANIA
Compani De Librarii Bucuresti S.A.
Str. Lipscani no. 26, sector 3
Bucharest
Tel: (40 1) 613 9645
Fax: (40 1) 312 4000

RUSSIAN FEDERATION
Isdatelstvo <Ves Mir>
9a, Kolpachniy Pereulok
Moscow 101831
Tel: (7 095) 917 87 49
Fax: (7 095) 917 92 59

SINGAPORE; TAIWAN, CHINA; MYANMAR; BRUNEI
Ashgate Publishing Asia Pacific Pte. Ltd.
41 Kallang Pudding Road #04-03
Golden Wheel Building
Singapore 349316
Tel: (65) 741-5166
Fax: (65) 742-9356
E-mail: ashgate@asianconnect.com

SLOVENIA
Gospodarski Vestnik Publishing Group
Dunajska cesta 5
1000 Ljubljana
Tel: (386 61) 133 83 47; 132 12 30
Fax: (386 61) 133 80 30
E-mail: repansekj@gvestnik.si

SOUTH AFRICA, BOTSWANA
For single titles:
Oxford University Press Southern Africa
Vasco Boulevard, Goodwood
P.O. Box 12119, N1 City 7463
Cape Town
Tel: (27 21) 595 4400
Fax: (27 21) 595 4430
E-mail: oxford@oup.co.za

For subscription orders:
International Subscription Service
P.O. Box 41095
Craighall
Johannesburg 2024
Tel: (27 11) 880-1448
Fax: (27 11) 880-6248
E-mail: iss@is.co.za

SPAIN
Mundi-Prensa Libros, S.A.
Castello 37
28001 Madrid
Tel: (34 1) 431-3399
Fax: (34 1) 575-3998
E-mail: libreria@mundiprensa.es

Mundi-Prensa Barcelona
Consell de Cent, 391
08009 Barcelona
Tel: (34 3) 488-3492
Fax: (34 3) 487-7659
E-mail: barcelona@mundiprensa.es

SRI LANKA, THE MALDIVES
Lake House Bookshop
100, Sir Chittampalam Gardiner Mawatha
Colombo 2
Tel: (94 1) 32105

Fax: (94 1) 432104
E-mail: LHL@sri.lanka.net

SWEDEN
Wennergren-Williams AB
P.O. Box 1305
S-171 25 Solna
Tel: (46 8) 705-97-50
Fax: (46 8) 27-00-71
E-mail: mail@wwi.se

SWITZERLAND
Librairie Payot Service Institutionnel
Côtes-de-Montberon 30
1002 Lausanne
Tel: (41 21) 341-3229
Fax: (41 21) 341-3235

ADECO Van Diermen EditionsTechniques
Ch. de Lacuez 41
CH1807 Blonay
Tel: (41 21) 943 2673
Fax: (41 21) 943 3605

THAILAND
Central Books Distribution
306 Silom Road
Bangkok 10500
Tel: (66 2) 235-5400
Fax: (66 2) 237-8321

TRINIDAD & TOBAGO AND THE CARRIBBEAN
Systematics Studies Ltd.
St. Augustine Shopping Center
Eastern Main Road, St. Augustine
Trinidad & Tobago, West Indies
Tel: (868) 645-8466
Fax: (868) 645-8467
E-mail: tobe@trinidad.net

UGANDA
Gustro Ltd.
PO Box 9997, Madhvani Building
Plot 16/4 Jinja Rd.
Kampala
Tel: (256 41) 251 467
Fax: (256 41) 251 468
E-mail: wbank@swiftuganda.com

UNITED KINGDOM
Microinfo Ltd.
P.O. Box 3, Alton, Hampshire GU34 2PG
England
Tel: (44 1420) 86848
Fax: (44 1420) 89889
E-mail: wbank@ukminfo.demon.co.uk

The Stationery Office
51 Nine Elms Lane
London SW8 5DR
Tel: (44 171) 873-8400
Fax: (44 171) 873-8242

VENEZUELA
Tecni-Ciencia Libros, S.A.
Centro Cuidad Comercial Tamanco
Nivel C2, Caracas
Tel: (58 2) 959 5547; 5035; 0016
Fax: (58 2) 959 5636

ZAMBIA
University Bookshop, University of Zambia
Great East Road Campus
P.O. Box 32379
Lusaka
Tel: (260 1) 252 576
Fax: (260 1) 253 952

ZIMBABWE
Academic and Baobab Books (Pvt.) Ltd.
4 Conald Road, Graniteside
P.O. Box 567
Harare
Tel: 263 4 755035
Fax: 263 4 781913